Competitiveness Through Strategic Success

Peter H. Antoniou
Pomegranate International Co.

The Planning Forum
Oxford, Ohio

ISBN 0-7863-0311-5

Published by The Planning Forum, 5500
College Corner Pike, Oxford, Ohio 45056.

Printed in the United States of America

1 2 3 4 5 6 7 8 9 0 DOC 1 0 9 8 7 6 5 4

To My Parents

Foreword

This book presents the results of pioneering doctoral dissertation research by Peter H. Antoniou, addressed to providing empirical proof of the *Strategic Success Hypothesis* which I published in 1979.

The hypothesis claims that "bottom line" success of firms (and other environment-serving organizations) is highly correlated to the degree of alignment between the level of turbulence in the firm's environment, the strategic aggressiveness of the firms' behavior in the environment, and the openness to the environment of the firms' management capability (particularly openness of the top management).

Peter's research offers a statistically significant proof of this hypothesis. This research, completed in 1986, was followed by seven other doctoral dissertations, each of which tested the *Strategic Success Hypothesis* in different types of organizations (American not-for-profit; banks in the United Arab Emirates; parastatal firms in Algeria; small banks in San Diego, California; large United States banks; United States savings and loan banks; and business firms in Indonesia). All of these research efforts confirm and reinforce Peter's findings and their diversity offers proof that the *Strategic Success Hypothesis* is valid across a spectrum of economic-cultural-political settings and a spectrum of organizations serving different environments. The results obtained by Peter and his colleagues shed light on the currently vital problem of competitiveness confronting American firms.

As the above shows, the *Strategic Success Hypothesis* casts grave doubts on the validity of prescriptions for regaining competitiveness which offer the same solution to all firms in all industries. Our research shows that such prescriptions are likely to be valid at a particular level of environmental turbulence and become progressively invalid and dangerous at different levels of turbulence.

Our research also shows that a major determinant of competitiveness is the match of a firm's strategy to the firm's environment. Another major determinant of success is the match of the firm's management capability to strategy.

Our research shows that in the absence of this dual strategic match, efforts to regain competitiveness through cost reduction, increased competitive aggressiveness, and "return to basics," will not be sufficient.

H. Igor Ansoff

About the Author

Peter H. Antoniou, M.I.B.A., D.B.A., is a management professor and president of Pomegranate International, a firm involved in international trade, educational programs and consulting activities. In international trade, Pomegranate International matches buyers' and sellers' demand, negotiates joint venture agreements, and establishes international distributorship contracts.

Dr. Antoniou has been going to the Peoples' Republic of China on the invitation and under the auspices of the Foreign Affairs Office, to deliver seminars on international trade, strategy, and policy. These efforts lead to arranging for groups of executives and government officials from the PRC to come to the United States to attend seminars and develop business contacts. These organized educational activities have been positively received by both the PRC and the U.S. governments and currently serve one out of every five executives coming to the United States.

Dr. Antoniou consults in Europe, Mexico and China. Some of the companies he has worked with are IBM-Mexico, Johnson Wax, Infotec and Yanji Petrochemical Company. As mentioned above, he works directly with a number of Chinese companies to expand their international business and identify suitable working partners. In February 1993, he was given the Honorable Citizen Award in Guangzhou, China.

Dr. Antoniou is the founder and co-chair of the International Trade Committee of the Mid San Fernando Valley Chamber of Commerce in Los Angeles, which serves an area with more than 10,000 manufacturers.

Dr. Antoniou's book, *Challenges and Rewards of Exporting to the United States,* has been translated into Chinese and published in China under the sponsorship of the Foreign Economic Relations and Trade Commission of Shandong Province. It has been translated into Bulgarian and Greek. His latest book, Negotiating With Americans, will be translated and published in Gansu Province, China. His bi-monthly column on U.S.-China trade issues is published in the Development News of Tianjin.

Acknowledgements

I would like to express my sincere thanks and appreciation to Professor H. Igor Ansoff for his introduction and to recognize him as the inspiration for this work.

Dr. George Sawyer made this publication possible, initially by identifying its potential, and later, by actively encouraging its completion under difficult circumstances.

To Nicole Rae Brown who supported me toward the realization of this project, thank you.

I wish to give my special thanks to Katherine Whitman for her endless researching and editing. Her continuous questioning of issues and concepts helped in the construction and clarity of the ideas presented. Without this assistance, the editing and redefining process would have been interminable.

Preface

This is a book about the best way to run your company. It leaves no excuse for a company to operate with a bad strategy.

For best results, the level of the company's strategy must match the level of competence of its management, as well as the level of turbulence in the environment in which the company operates.

The following chapters present a statistically validated procedure for determining these levels, plus instructions on how to use this procedure, and on the correction of mismatches that would otherwise impair corporate performance.

THE INTENDED AUDIENCE

This study is for readers interested in selecting better strategies, in the practical systematic management of adaptation, and for everyone who has responsibility for managing and implementing company strategy.

More precisely, this book seeks to describe in simple and concrete language the concepts, facts, ideas, processes and procedures concerning company strategy that managers at all levels should know. Company strategy is interwoven within the entire process of management; thus, all managers should understand its nature and how it affects their position. Because some managers are unclear about what company strategic behavior is, they do not appreciate its importance. Others are unaware of the potential benefits to them or their firm of using the process, while still others who are unaware of corporate strategy are not convinced of its value.

This book aims to provide all managers with a practical, clear and complete understanding of what company strategy is, what its significance is, how well the strategy of a given company fits its capability and environment, and how best to implement and manage a strategy.

A manager concerned with assuring a promising future for his firm will find that this book provides a conceptual framework for managing discontinuities. Further, it provides a systematic approach for making strategic decisions.

A corporate planner will find a critical evaluation and practical application for the implementation of strategic analysis procedures and techniques. The planners' field of competence will be extended beyond strategic management by learning concepts and techniques of capability management and strategic implementation.

A person involved in corporate management will find this book informative, for the reader will realize the different steps and approaches management takes in decision making. Also, an individual will see how his position affects and is affected by discontinuity, and how he himself influences the situation.

A researcher will find the work enlightening in its approach, through the interrelationships demonstrated in the theories presented, and through the practical applications of the results. This study is for readers interested in selecting more effective strategies for their companies.

More precisely, this book seeks to describe in simple and concrete language the optimum relationship between management capability, the strategy being employed, and the degree of turbulence of the various environments in which that strategy must operate.

This book aims at providing all managers with a practical, clear and complete understanding of how well the strategy of a given company fits its capability and environment, and what to do if the fit is poor. The procedures presented were validated in a study detailed here, and were tested against eight different groups of actual companies in several industries in several different countries. The conclusions were confirmed as statistically significant

List of Figures and Tables

Table of Contents

INTRODUCTION

This is a book about how companies can improve their financial performance. To improve their performance they must match the aggressiveness of their strategy to their management capability, as well as to the level of turbulence in their environment—as concluded from a primary study followed by eight confirmatory studies. The primary study, discussed in the next several chapters, was based on analysis of 59 companies that had been described in a case study format. Business environment, strategy, and management capability affect financial performance, and this study analyzed the influence of these variables.

The basic premise with which this book begins is that an organization has a variety of structural forms and organizational processes from which to choose, and that these structural forms are not equally effective in implementing a given business strategy. Therefore, organization members should allocate time and effort to plan their organizational form, just as time and effort are allocated to the formulation of strategic and other plans.

Other design variables should be considered in addition to structure if a firm is to utilize its resources effectively and implement its strategy. The organization must be designed to facilitate the proper selection, training and development of its people. Individuals must be able to perform their tasks, and collectively the organization must have the capability required to carry out the desired strategy. That strategy should be consistent with the environment within which the organization operates.

The response of the organization should be in direct line with the needs of the surrounding environment. Hence, the choice of organizational form should be made only after a comprehensive design of the organization's strategy and systems. Information must also be available to direct, control and coordinate activities, and to measure performance effectively. The major design variables analyzed in this book are represented schematically in Figure I-1.

The significance of this work lies in the fact that it specifies the relationship between environment, strategy and capability, and demonstrates how this relationship affects a company's performance. Chapter One sets the stage by presenting the

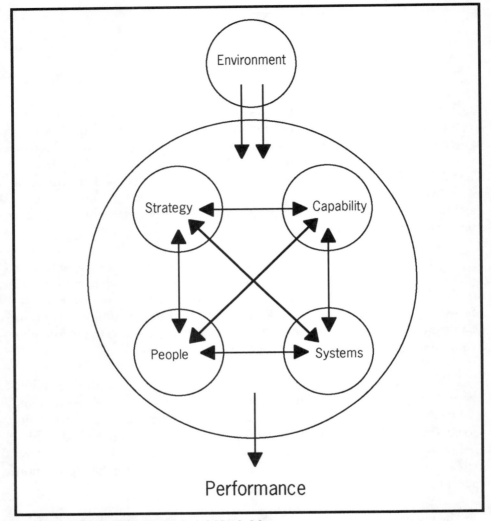

Figure I.1: The Examined Variables

different attributes measured for each organization and how they are interrelated, as well as the research questions for the study. Chapter Two contains the methods used to process and analyze the data. Chapter Three presents the results of the study following the research question sequence. Chapter Four summarizes the findings and their significance. Chapter Five discusses practical applications—how to approach the variables and their relationships in a business setting, because the findings of this study provide a practical guide that can assist business practitioners in improving company financial performance. Chapter Six includes a review of relevant literature pertaining to the theoretical basis for this study and summarizes the results of the eight confirmatory studies on different groups of companies in different industries and countries.

DEFINITIONS

Throughout this study the following definitions will be employed:

1. **Capability** is the management competence, capacity, and ability of the units charged with general management responsibilities. For effective operation the selected level of thrust at which the organization operates must be supported by an equivalent *capability*, defined in terms of culture, managerial competence, the management system, availability of information, the corporate structure, and distribution of power.

2. **Environment** is the atmosphere within which the organization operates. It is characterized by its turbulence, defined in terms of speed and novelty of change. Turbulence of the environment is its level of changeability, the *discontinuity* of the events *combined* with the *speed* at which they surface and develop.

3. **Strategy** defines the scope of the firms' operations, the strategic thrust of the organization, and the deployment of resources to make the whole organization a competitive enterprise. Successful organizations develop a strategic thrust, defined in terms of marketing and innovation, appropriate for the level of turbulence in which the organization operates.

4. **Systems** are the formal methods for getting information into an organization, selecting appropriate strategic goals and conducting managerial problem solving. Systems also include structure, information and planning.

5. **People** are the human element of the organization, without which it cannot operate; though expandable, changeable and adjustable, this element includes the culture, mentality and qualifications of people.

6. **Performance** is the financial performance of the organization measured via the following distinct ratios:
    1. net profit to net sales
    2. net sales to net worth
    3. net profit to net worth

These ratios were selected because they indicated the operating efficiency and strategic effectiveness of the companies analyzed, and because they were the only ratios from which the comparative measures could be obtained for the performance of the industries to which the companies studied belonged. The comparative measures were obtained from Dun & Bradstreet's *Key Business Ratios* (1965-1985).

The ratio of *net profit to net sales* was obtained by dividing net earnings of the business, after taxes, by net sales (the dollar volume less returns, allowances and cash discounts). The ratio indicates the operating efficiency of the company by showing how well the company is run—how well the firm's management utilizes the firm's sales, production and distribution toward maximizing the company's profits.

The ratio of *net sales to net worth* was obtained by dividing the company's tangible net worth by sales. Tangible net worth is the equity of stockholders in the business, obtained by subtracting total liabilities from total assets. This ratio provides information about operating efficiency and strategic effectiveness by giving a measure of relative turnover of invested capital. In other words, it measures the sales and operation of the firm, as well as the company's use of its financial resources to respond to customer needs.

The ratio of *net profit to net worth* was derived from the multiplication of the first two ratios and provides information on the overall effectiveness and efficiency of the firm. It provides information on how effectively a firm utilizes its financial resources to earn a profit. It identifies the efficiency of the operation and the effectiveness of the strategy adopted by the firm.

7. The **Instrument** used is an analytical procedure developed by H. I. Ansoff and discussed in detail in Appendix A. Ansoff's procedure is an excellent *instrument* for the type of analysis on which this study is based, because it is designed to measure and match environment, strategy, and capability.

8. **Gap.** The hypothesis underlying this work and confirmed by its results is that, for best financial results, the aggressiveness of management strategy, the capability of management, and the turbulence of the environment must be at the same levels; if they are not, then there is a *gap* between where they are and where they need to be if best financial results are to be achieved. Much of the analysis deals with the size and nature of the gaps that exist for each company.

Chapter 1
ABOUT THE STUDY

The primary study described in this book explores the relationships between business environment, strategy, and capability in a series of companies in order to answer the following questions:

How does environment relate to strategy and capability?
How is company performance affected by environment, strategy and capability?
How is continued successful financial performance achieved?
Does company financial performance correlate with the corporate strategic profile at different levels of environmental turbulence?

Before these questions could be answered, diagnostic measurements were necessary for each company concerning:

- the environmental turbulence.
- the aggressiveness of the firm's strategy.
- the firm's management capability profile.
- the firm's financial performance.

Of 163 companies analyzed, 59 met the selection criteria and were used as the basis for this study. These were U.S. companies; 43 were in manufacturing (172-3811 SIC code) and 16 were wholesale/retail companies (5013-5712 SIC code). The selection criteria were based on the company's business environment, strategy and capability, plus availability of the required financial data. Each selected company was public at the time of analysis. SIC classifications were based on "the business we are in," as described in the case study. All companies belonged to a single SIC classification, and 70 percent or more of their business activities were within that classification. If a company was a subsidiary of another corporation, only the data for the subsidiary or division was collected and analyzed. The companies operated within the same SIC category for the duration of the study, and the research data for the study was based on information gathered until 1985. The information included data on company performance, industry performance and business environment for the four-year period each company was analyzed.

Company data used in the analysis was not all from the same four-year time span, but rather spread across 12 years. This strengthens the findings because similar performance for the examined companies was observed through time.

The statistics used in the study were the count, mean, standard deviation and the significance at the 0.05 confidence level, as determined by the Mann-Whitney U Test.

RESEARCH QUESTION

The research question posed for this study was: **How does the corporate strategic profile relate to environmental turbulence, as measured by company financial performance?** Analysis of this question led to the definition of four sub-questions:

1. Is there a gap between environmental turbulence and strategic aggressiveness?

2. Is there a gap between environmental turbulence and the general management capability necessary to respond to this turbulence?

3. Is there a gap between environmental turbulence and strategic aggressiveness in combination with general management capability?

4. What is the correlation between 1, 2, and 3 respectively and the financial performance of the firm?

The conclusion, as will be discussed in detail: **When environment, strategy and capability are on the same level (of a five-point scale), the company's financial performance will be optimal. When there is a gap between the levels of the variables, financial performance declines.**

INSTRUMENTATION

The data was collected utilizing H. I. Ansoff's procedure for analysis (see Appendix A), referred to here as the *instrument*. The procedure matches environment, strategy and capability. Three distinct parts of the procedure individually assess these variables. The purpose of the first section is to assess the turbulence of the firm's environment; two tables constructed with a total of 15 attributes present a profile of environmental turbulence. The data was classified into five levels of turbulence:

repetitive, expanding, changing, discontinuous and surpriseful. The first level, repetitive, represents an environment with low turbulence, while level five, surpriseful, represents one with high turbulence or high variability.

The aggressiveness of the firm's strategy is identified in the second section of the instrument. This section contains two tables with a total of 15 attributes and a five-point classification from stable to creative. The five levels of aggressiveness of the strategy are: stable, reactive, changing, exploring and creative. Level one, stable, represents a low level, and level five, creative, a high level of strategic aggressiveness. These five levels correspond to the ones identifying the turbulence of the environment.

In the third section of the instrument, the internal functions of the firm determine the firm's general capability profile based on six components: culture, managers, structure, systems, management technology and management capability. Twenty-five attributes are classified within these six components. The capability profile scale includes: custodial, production, marketing, strategic and flexible. These classifications match the previously proposed scales, with level one representing a low-, and five, a high-level capability profile. Figure 1-1 illustrates the five corresponding levels of environment, strategy, and capability.

The information for each company was analyzed by applying the instrument and classifying the information according to the scale for each individual variable. The instrument provided identification of the specifics necessary to classify each firm. A detailed analysis of a sample company, the way it was analyzed, and the identification of the types of gap it showed is presented in Appendix B.

The company analysis followed these steps:

1. The information for each individual company was examined to identify whether it fulfilled the general criteria.

2. The company was analyzed further to classify its attributes as required by the individual parts of the instrument.

3. Preliminary financial data on company performance was collected.

4. A complete analysis followed, reviewing earlier classifications and filling in all possible parts of the instrument.

Strategic Posture Analysis

	1 REPETITIVE	2 EXPANDING	3 CHANGING	4 DISCONTINUOUS	5 SURPRISEFUL
Levels of Environmental Turbulence	Repetitive	Slow Incremental Forecastable	Fast Incremental Forecastable	Discontinuous Predictable	Discontinuous Partially Predictable
Aggressiveness of Strategy	STABLE — Stable Based on Precedents	REACTIVE — Reactive Based on Experience	ANTICIPATORY — Anticipatory Based on Extrapolation	EXPLORING — Based on New Observable Alternatives	CREATIVE — Novel, Based on Creativity
Openness of Capability	CUSTODIAL — Rejects Change	PRODUCTION — Adopts to Change	MARKETING — Seeks Familiar Change Synergistic	STRATEGIC — Seeks Related Change Global	FLEXIBLE — Seeks Novel Change Creative

H. Igor Ansoff, Implanting Strategic Management (1984: 216)

Figure 1.1: Strategic Posture Analysis

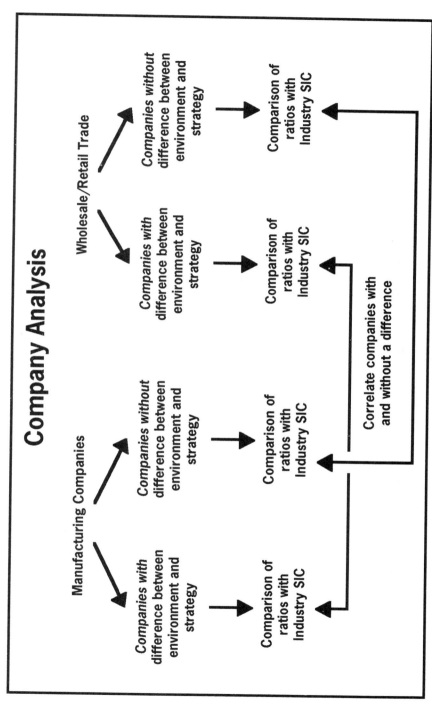

Figure 1.2: Procedural Analysis of Companies With and Without Gap Between Environment and Strategy for Manufacturing and Wholesale/Retail Trade Companies.

5. Financial information was collected on the company from the analysis itself and from *Moody's Industrial Manual.*

6. Financial information was collected on the industry sector the company belonged to from Dun & Bradstreet's *Key Business Ratios.*

7. A profile of the overall company posture was identified by plotting the results on Figure A-3 of the instrument to illustrate balance between environment, strategy and capability. (See Appendix A.)

8. The four-year arithmetic average financial performance for the company was calculated, as well as the average for the industry to which the company belonged.

9. The manufacturing and wholesale/retail trade companies were separated.

10. Within each industry group, the companies were separated according to which of the three types of gap they showed: 1) between environment and strategy, 2) between environment and capability, or 3) between environment and strategy in combination with capability.

11. The count, mean and standard deviation were calculated for the three different types of gap and for each industry group.

12. The Mann-Whitney U Test was used to identify the relationship and level of significance between the analyzed factors.

Figure 1.2 illustrates the pattern of company analysis that examined the relationship between environment and strategy.

The same procedure was used for all three different groupings of data:

1. Environment versus strategy.
2. Environment versus capability.
3. Environment versus strategy in combination with capability.

Chapter 2
ANALYSIS OF DATA

This chapter describes the procedure for analysis of data after the instrument was applied to each individual company to identify and measure any gap between the variables.

IDENTIFICATION OF THE EXISTENCE OF A GAP

The instrument allowed the identification of the level of environmental turbulence, aggressiveness of the firm's strategy and general management capability. This information gathered was entered in Figures A-3 and B-3 of the instrument (see Appendices A and B).

Figure A-3 allows the representation of the data, derived from the instrument, in a single convenient form. It is based on the same five-point scale of analysis of environment, strategy and capability, from stable to creative; in other words, from a low to a high level of turbulence.

Companies were grouped in one of two categories: companies having a gap and those without one. Companies were categorized as having a gap if there were one or more points of difference on the five points of scale. That is, in examining the existence of a gap between environment and strategy, if the result for environment was anticipating (level 3), and for strategy was either exploring (level 4) or reactive (level 2), then the company was recorded as having a gap between environment and strategy. On the other hand, companies with no gap were classified in this category if there was less than one point of difference between the examined variables. That is, in examining the existence of a gap between environment and strategy, if the result for environment was anticipating (level 3), and for strategy was also anticipating (level 3), the company was recorded as having no gap between environment and strategy.

FINANCIAL ANALYSIS OF DATA

The following three ratios were used in the study: *sales over net worth, net profit over sales,* and *profit to net worth.* For each company, the four-year average was calculated and compared with the average of the same four-year period for the industry to which the company belonged. This allowed comparison of the company's performance with that of the industry, to see whether the company was doing better or worse than the industry for that four-year period. The mean and standard deviation were similarly calculated for every group of data.

STATISTICAL ANALYSIS OF DATA

The mean, standard deviation and Mann-Whitney U Test were utilized in the study. The calculations were performed for the three types of gaps examined in this study: (a) between environment and strategy, (b) between environment and capability, and (c) between environment and strategy in combination with capability. The steps listed below were followed in analyzing the data:

1. Comparison of the performance of the company with the appropriate industry, utilizing the ratios *sales to net worth* and *net profit to sales*.

2. Comparison of the mean performance of the companies in the same industry with and without a gap.

3. Comparison of the mean of companies with that of the industry to identify: (a) companies performing better or worse than the industry and (b) the performance of companies with and without a gap for each type of gap.

4. The level of significance of the results was computed by utilizing the Mann-Whitney U Test.

5. Comparison of the mean and standard deviation for each company performing better and worse than the industry to which it belongs.

6. The overall performance, efficiency, and effectiveness of the firms was calculated by multiplying the mean of the difference between companies and their industry.

7. The results of the financial data were analyzed and correlated between the two industry groups (manufacturing and wholesale/retail companies) in order to identify the relationship between the two.

8. The percentage of the companies performing better and worse than the industry was calculated.

The data was collected and analyzed with a .05 percent confidence level. Accuracy was held to 15 decimal points for all calculations. The sample means and standard deviation calculated were unbiased estimators of the evaluating means and the evaluating standard deviation.

Chapter 3
RESULTS

This chapter details the results of the study of environment, strategy, capability and financial performance of 59 selected companies. The research question for this study was: **How does the corporate strategic profile relate to environmental turbulence, as measured by company financial performance?**

The research question was broken down into four subquestions:

1. Is there a gap between environmental turbulence and strategic aggressiveness?

2. Is there a gap between environmental turbulence and the general management capability necessary to respond to this turbulence?

3. Is there a gap between environmental turbulence and strategic aggressiveness in combination with general management capability?

4. What is the correlation between 1, 2, and 3 respectively, and the financial performance of the firm?

The study compared the performance of each company to the industry to which it belongs. The presentation of the results follows the same breakdown as above.

The results of the ratios *sales to net worth* and *net profit to sales* were presented first, followed by the results of the ratio *net profit to net worth*. Bar graphs for the first two ratios in Figures 3.1 and 3.2 illustrate companies performing better or worse than the average for the industry. All companies to the left of the x axis performed worse than the industry (negative figures) and all companies on the right performed better than the industry (positive figures).

SUBQUESTION 1

Is there a gap between environment and strategy?

Yes—such a gap can often be identified. A significant number of companies were found with and without gaps between environment and strategy. Also, in analyzing the ratio *sales to net worth,* companies were found that performed better and worse than the average performance of the industry.

Within the group performing better and the group performing worse than the industry, there were companies with a gap and companies without one. Out of the 59 companies observed, 24 were identified as having a gap. Companies with no gap performed better in both groups. Figure 3.1 illustrates companies performing worse than the average industry.

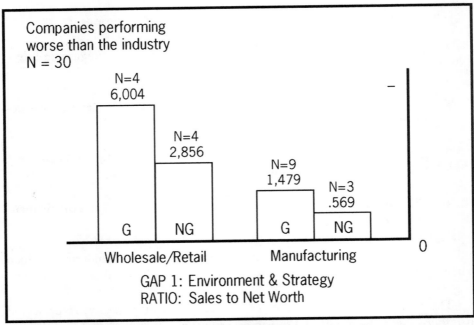

Figure 3.1: Companies With and Without a Gap Between Environment and Strategy Performing Worse than the Industry (Sales to Net Worth Ratio)

Companies with no gap had distinctly better performance than those with a gap in both industry sectors. In other words, companies without a gap were the best of the worst wholesale/retail and manufacturing companies.

Figure 3.2 illustrates companies performing better than the industry. As stated previously, companies with no gap performed better than companies with one.

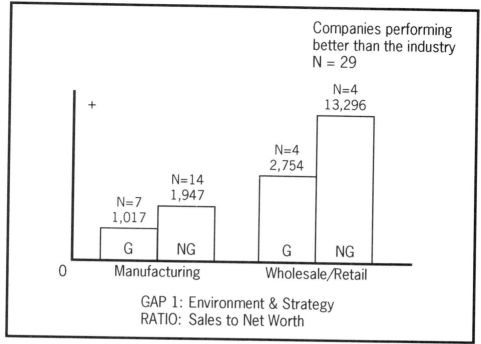

Figure 3.2: Companies With and Without a Gap Between Environment and Strategy Performing Better than the Industry (Sales to Net Worth Ratio)

The very same findings were evident when the ratio *profit to sales* was calculated. In this case, companies without a gap had better financial performance than those with a gap, as shown in Figure 3.3.

In this section, three companies had a gap which shifted during the period of the study from below average to performing better than the industry average.

SUBQUESTION 2

Is there a gap between environmental turbulence and the general management capability necessary to respond to this turbulence?

Again a gap can be identified. Companies without a gap performed comparatively better than those with a gap under all circumstances. Figure 3.4 illustrates the findings of the ratio *sales to net worth* for companies with and without a gap for that ratio.

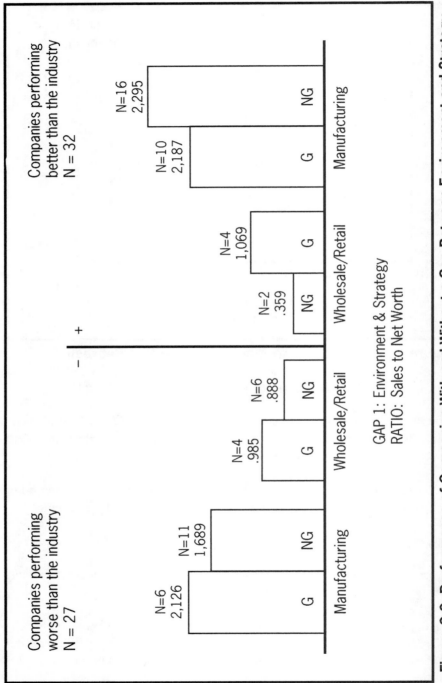

Figure 3.3: Performance of Companies With and Without a Gap Between Environment and Strategy (Sales to Net Worth Ratio)

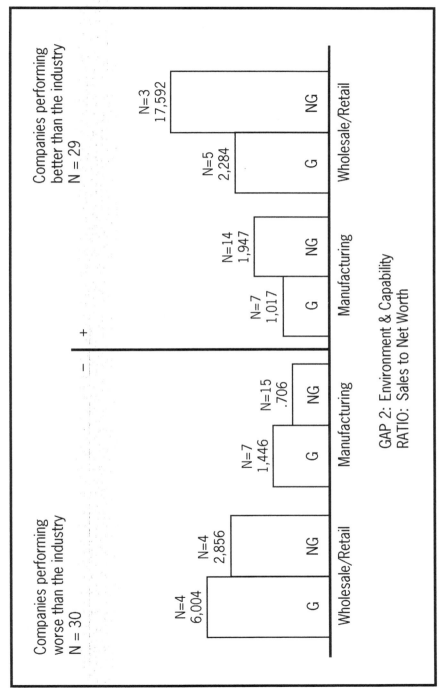

Figure 3.4: Performance of Companies With and Without a Gap Between Environment and Capability (Sales to Net Worth Ratio)

Identical findings were reached while analyzing the ratio *profit to net sales* in Figure 3.5. A peculiarity was observed in the analysis of this ratio. In the group of companies performing worse than the industry, manufacturing companies with no gap performed worse than manufacturing companies with a gap. Also, in the group of companies performing better than the average of the industry, wholesale/retail companies with a gap performed better than those without a gap. In other words, in the two groupings of data, there were companies with gaps performing better than companies without them.

Subquestion 3

Is there a gap between environmental turbulence and strategic aggressiveness in combination with general management capability?

In response to the third subquestion, a gap was identified, and companies without a gap were found to perform comparatively better than companies with one. The findings for the ratio *sales to net worth* are illustrated in Figure 3.6. In all instances, companies without a gap performed better than those with one.

A total of 29 companies were identified as having no gap in this group, out of which 15 performed better and 14 performed worse than the industry to which they belonged. Companies with no gap were better performers within their industry than those with a gap. In the group performing worse than the industry, companies with no gap were the best of the worst.

Figure 3.7 illustrates the findings of the *profit to sales* ratio. In two out of four groups of data, companies without a gap performed better than those with one.

Overall Company Performance

Most important are the overall performance figures. In all cases for the ratio *sales to net worth,* and in all but five cases for the ratio *profit to sales,* companies without a gap performed better than companies with a gap.

The ratio *profit to net worth* was calculated next. This ratio illustrates the overall efficiency and effectiveness of the firm's financial performance, since it deals with the impact of the company's profit on the company's net worth. See Table 3.1 for an illustration of the results by type of gap and type of industry.

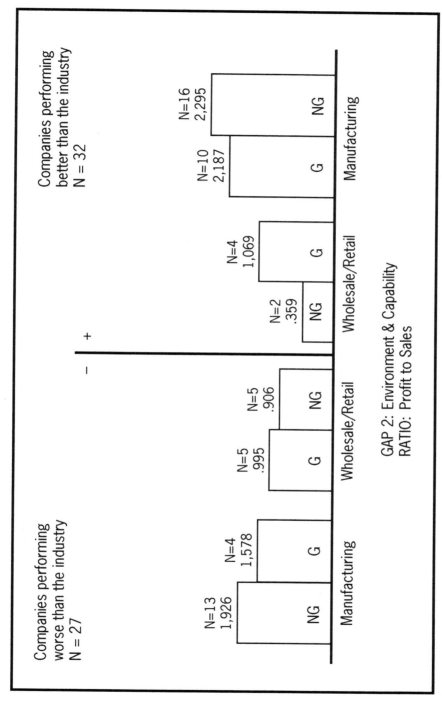

Figure 3.5: Performance of Companies With and Without a Gap Between Environment and Capability (Profit to Sales Ratio)

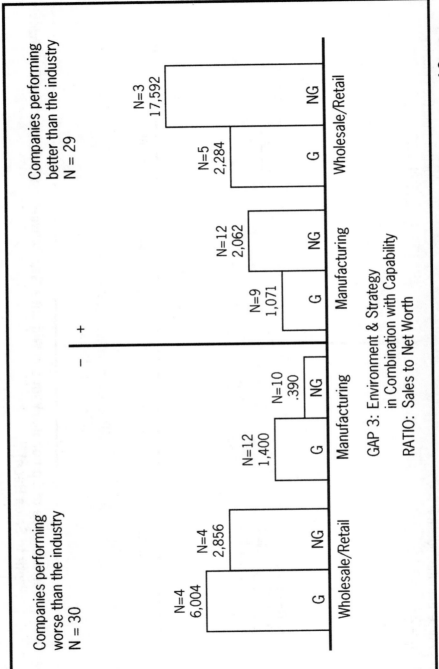

Figure 3.6: Performance of Companies With and Without a Gap Between Environment and Strategy in Combination with Capability (Sales to Net Worth Ratio)

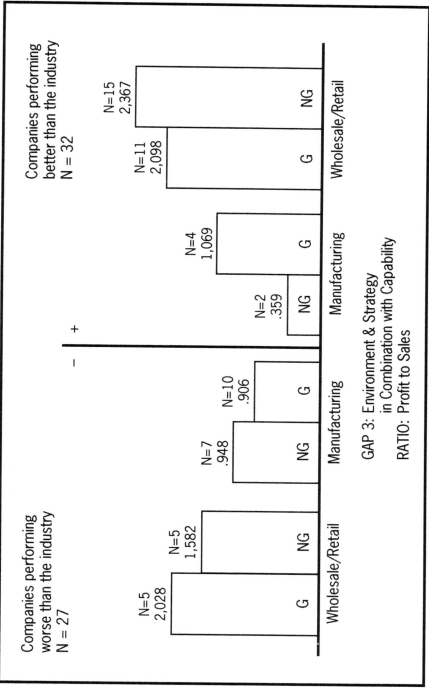

Figure 3.7: Performance of Companies With and Without a Gap Between Environment and Strategy in Combination with Capability (Profit to Sales Ratio)

	W/R–G	N	M–G	N	M–NG	N	W/R–NG	N	Total N
G1	8.835	8	11.370	16	17.634	27	27.005	8	59
G2	9.971	9	13.198	14	16.111	29	28.097	7	59
G3	9.971	9	10.175	21	20.822	22	28.097	7	59

Gap 1: Environment and Strategy   W/R: Wholesale/Retail Companies
Gap 2: Environment and Capability   M: Manufacturing Companies
Gap 3: Environment and Strategy in   G: Companies With Gap
     Combination With Capability   NG: Companies With No Gap
     N: Number of Companies

Table 3.1: Performance of Companies With and Without a Gap for All Three Types of Gap (Profit to Net Worth Ratio)

The results identify some substantial differences between the performance of companies. More specifically, in gap 1 the difference between wholesale/retail companies with and without gap was (27.005 - 8.835 =) 17.17 ratio points in favor of companies without a gap. In other words, wholesale/retail companies without a gap performed three times better than the ones with a gap. In all groups of data, companies with no gap performed better than companies with a gap regardless of the type of industry or type of gap.

CORRELATION OF FINDINGS

The Mann-Whitney U Test was conducted next. All companies, whether manufacturing or wholesale/retail, performed in similar ways across the sample. The finding showed a significant correlation—up to 95 percent—where manufacturing and wholesale/retail showed similar behavior of performance. This specific finding allowed the sample to be examined as two groups, where a gap was the only differentiating factor. Thus, it enabled the comparison of performance for all companies with a gap and all companies without one.

The findings presented in Table 3.2 show that all companies without a gap performed better than companies with one. These findings were supported by a statistical analysis of the mean and standard deviation.

Additional insights about companies performing better and worse than the industry can be obtained by comparing the company's ratio *profit to net worth* with

	All Companies With Gap	N	All Companies With No Gap	N	Total N
G1	11.101	24	23.491	35	59
G2	12.867	23	27.120	36	59
G3	10.648	30	27.600	29	59

Gap 1: Environment and Strategy
Gap 2: Environment and Capability
Gap 3: Environment and Strategy in Combination With Capability

Table 3.2: Comparison of Performance of Companies With and Without a Gap

that of the industry. The ratio *profit to net worth,* or ROI, gives us a good indication of the well-being of the company.

This table is based on the ratio *profits to net worth*, defined as the equity of the stockholders in the business, as obtained by subtracting total liabilities from total assets and then deducting intangibles. The ratio is obtained by dividing net profits after taxes by tangible net worth.

$$\frac{sales}{net\ worth} \quad x \quad \frac{net\ profit}{sales} \quad or\ ROI$$

When we compare the ratio ROI for the company to the ROI of the industry, the results should be above 1 for companies performing better than the industry, and below 1 for those companies performing worse than the industry (see Figure 3.8). Of the total of 30 companies with a gap, 56.7 percent performed worse than the industry, and the best performers were 3.5 times the industry average. On the other hand, out of 29 companies without a gap, 34.5 percent performed below industry standards, and the best performers were 8.6 times the industry average. There were 10.4 percent of companies with no gap that performed over and above the highest point of 3.5 times the industry average for companies with a gap. This is another indication that companies without a gap performed better than companies with one.

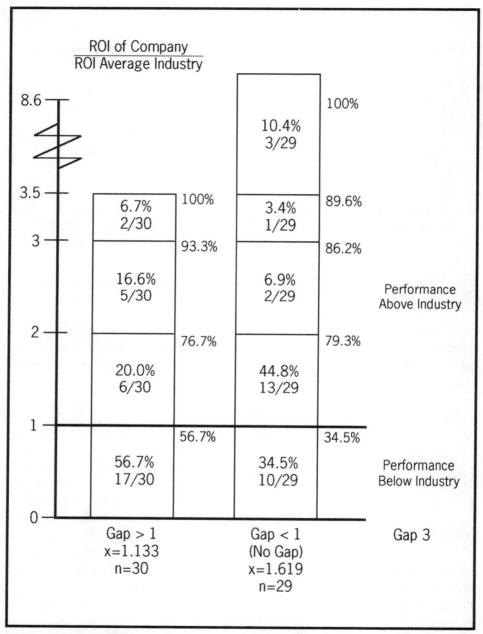

Figure 3.8: Comparison of Performance of Companies With and Without a Gap Between Environment and Strategy in Combination With Capability

Chapter 4
FINDINGS

This chapter summarizes the findings of the primary study which are also valid for the eight supporting studies summarized in Chapter 6. The findings of the primary study are as follows:

1. The environment is believed to be the leading indicator of the strategy a company needs, and the Ansoff procedure allows identification of the level of environmental turbulence.

2. This instrument also allows identification of the level of aggressiveness of the firm's strategy plus the level of capability of general management.

3. While utilizing this instrument, it was found that it is possible to identify any difference between two of these three variables; that is, to identify the existence of any gap between environment, strategy and capability.

4. In analyzing the different types of gaps, companies without a gap between (I) *environment and strategy*, (II) *environment and capability*, or (III) *environment and strategy in combination with capability* performed financially better than companies with a gap. These findings partially support Ansoff's adapted hypothesis that companies whose strategic profile is not significantly different from the firm's environment performed better than the companies whose profile was significantly different.

5. These findings were true for companies performing better or worse than the average of the industry to which they belonged. In other words, when companies performed better than the industry to which they belonged, the companies *without a gap* between environment and corporate strategic profile performed better than the companies *with a gap* between the same attributes. When companies performed worse than the average performance of the industry to which they belonged, those companies *without a gap* performed *better* than those *with a gap*.

6.   While comparing the performance of companies with a gap and those with-
     out one, companies without a gap were found to financially outperform
     companies with one by more than 210 percent in the ratio *net profit to net
     worth* for all three types of gaps analyzed. More specifically:

Environment and strategy: Companies without a gap outperformed
companies with one by 211.6 percent.

Environment and capability: Companies without a gap outperformed
companies with one by 210.8 percent.

Environment and strategy in combination with capability: Companies without a gap outperformed those with one by 259.2 percent.

SIGNIFICANCE

The significance of this study lies in the fact that it validates a practical tool for
identifying the existing levels of environment, strategy, and capability (and the degree
to which they match), as well as establishing the importance of the measurement.
This tool facilitates the identification of a company's strengths and weaknesses, and
permits it to identify opportunity and to become aware of potential threats emerging from the business environment.

Companies were found that operate both with and without a gap between these
attributes. Companies with a gap are not as successful as those that do not have a
gap between the same attributes. There were more better-performing companies
having no gap than companies with one. On the other hand, more companies with
a gap performed worse than the average of the industry.

Another group of companies also was identified: companies that had an identified gap but performed better than companies without a gap. This appears to be
due to the impact of operating efficiency. Even though companies with a gap do
not have the same potential to become better performers, some were able to excel
due to strong management capability or operating efficiency. The management team
in this category was able to operate better than the comparable group of companies
having no gap. In turn, the management teams in companies without any gap were
operating inefficiently.

However, in the long run, companies without a gap have more potential for
improving financial performance.

Conclusions and Implications

This study found that manufacturing and wholesale/retail companies perform in similar ways, and have a similar response to the various types of gaps. Companies were observed whose behavior and management capability did not coincide with the level of environmental turbulence. In the majority of these cases, the environmental turbulence was on a higher level than the management capability. In only two cases was a gap observed where the environmental turbulence lagged behind the strategic aggressiveness and general management capability. Thus, the study found that when a gap exists, the corporate strategic profile generally lags behind environmental turbulence.

In those instances when the environment was lagging behind the strategic aggressiveness and general management capability, the companies performed better than the average of the industry to which they belonged.

This study found that companies without a significant difference between environmental turbulence and corporate strategic profile performed more successfully than companies with a significant difference between the same factors.

Chapter 5
WHAT SHOULD THE MANAGER DO?

The basic operating assumption is that a balance between environment, strategy and capability increases the likelihood of financial success.

Strategic management decisions are primarily focused on developing: (1) the master strategy, and (2) the implementation of this strategy. These decisions are based on answering the following questions:

1. What business are we really in?
2. Where are we now?
3. Where do we want to be?
4. How do we get there?

Provided that a company's mission statement is clear, top management can determine the firm's current position, thus allowing the company to formulate a master strategy. The master strategy should include the identification of opportunities and threats triggered by the environment. This way, the company could capitalize on its strengths and guard against its weaknesses. The current assessment of the environment is important since environment is the leading indicator of the way the company needs to act and react. Through the analysis of the environment, managers will be able to identify the marketing niches worth exploring, and to base company goals and objectives on it.

In analyzing the environment, firms must be aware of the phenomenon of myopia (Salameh, 1988). This occurs when a company analyzes the environment but views it to be different from the actual reality. An example of this would be when the firm views the changeability of the environment to be on level 2, but it is actually on level 3 or 4. This phenomenon occurs because of biased analysis. Therefore, caution should be taken in using and collecting information so as to make a correct interpretation of the state of the environment. One way to prevent biased analysis is by assimilating information about the positioning of the company within the environment from sources that are as unbiased as possible.

Based on the analysis of the environment, managers can determine desired objectives within the specific strategic business area (SBA). Attention can then be directed to internal strengths and weaknesses, and more specifically to strategy and capability.

The goal is to identify the internal level of operation for the strategy and capability of the firm. Items to be identified include the following:

Strategy items:	—	Competitive Posture
	—	Mission, Goals and Objectives
	—	Structure
Capability items:	—	Managers
	—	Culture
	—	Incentives
	—	Rewards
	—	Systems

When an internal analysis is completed, the manager will have a good idea where the firm stands. The next step is to compare the internal analysis with the external evaluation and identify the variance between them. There are five potential scenarios:

1. Environment = Strategy = Capability: This is the optimum scenario. Few companies are in this scenario; their main objective is continuous renewal to maintain this equality.

2. Environment = Capability ≠ Strategy: This is the best of the lesser scenarios. Usually this occurs during the process of reorganization.

3. Environment ≠ Strategy = Capability: Internally in line with strategy. There is a question of short-sightedness. Does the management experience myopia and misinterpretation of the true state of the environment?

4. Environment = Strategy ≠ Capability: High resistance, miscommunication. Management is tuned in with what needs to be done but no one else.

5. Environment ≠ Strategy ≠ Capability: Potential crisis. Especially when environment is at the highest level, and strategy and capability lag behind. Implementation of turnaround strategy is urgent.

These scenarios lead to two questions:

1.   *How can management analyze the internal and external factors?*
2.   *What can management do after they have analyzed the variables to facilitate optimum performance?*

The first question was discussed in Chapter 1; Ansoff (1977, 1984, 1990) developed an instrument which allows the identification of the level of environment, strategy and capability on a scale of one to five. Environment is determined through the analysis of 19 parameters for marketing and innovation turbulence; strategy is determined through the analysis of 16 parameters for marketing and innovation strategy; and capability is determined through 28 parameters for management, and climate and competence profiles.

As the analysis process is completed, it provides a corresponding average for each one of the attributes. A comparison of the findings on a cumulative index for all three attributes allows the identification of any gap, and the managers should decide how to correct any gap(s) found.

This leads to the second question. Management has already defined specific objectives through the environmental analysis, but there may be differences/gaps between the level of environmental turbulence and of strategic aggressiveness and/or capability. Which gap should be tackled first, and how? Environment is the leading indicator, setting the stage for the company's actions. Strategy aids the company in setting objectives and is the means to meet the realities of the environment achieved via capability. More specifically, strategy is formulated through the people element.

Employees should be made aware of the present condition and anticipated changes in the environment. In this way, the people element is part of the solution, and not part of the problem. Strategy will be the leading indicator as to what needs to be changed, and this change will be designed/found/implemented by people. The human element is needed to implement the new strategy within the existing and adjusted organizational structure and capability levels, not only to support the change, but to also be a part of triggering the changes in the environment.

To summarize briefly:

> *Environment embodies Change.*
> *Change is addressed via Strategy.*
> *Strategy is supported by Capability.*

Traditionally, environment was addressed by strategic moves followed by capability development, although sometimes time-lag made the response outdated. To address the question of time-lag, managers investigating environmental changes prepared the capability for anticipated changes simultaneously so that when the strategy was implemented, capability was in place to support it. But, the time span has further decreased. Since managers are generally removed from the fighting zone of day-to-day changes in the environment, changes in strategy and capability reach the point of occurring simultaneously, affecting one another in a dynamic form. The overall need is to anticipate change in the environment before it occurs, so strategy and capability are in place to address the evolved changes, all based on the mission of the company (which is based on answering the question of what business the company is really in, and by following the company's philosophy).

This sequence changes the job of the managers to be facilitators of change, rather than instigators of it.

Chapter 6

ISSUES AND THEORIES

The industrial revolution and the mass-production era gave rise to terms such as competition, infrastructure production, technology, organization, environmental turbulence, and product differentiation. During the industrial era, most of the major changes in the business environment originated from leading aggressive firms that established the style and pace of progess.

Ansoff (1987) presents an overview of the different stages of the development of an industry (see Figure 6.1).

INDUSTRY DEVELOPMENT			
Industrial Revolution	Production Oriented	Market Oriented	Post-Industrial
Birth of Entrepreneur	Mass Production	Mass Marketing	Environment Oriented
Creation of firm			

Figure 6.1: Phases of the Development of the Industry

The focal point of the industrial revolution era was the creation and development of the modern firm. The two sequential phases of the firms' development were mass production and mass marketing. Henry Ford presented the way of thinking for the mass production era best by saying, "One can have [a Model T] in any color as long as it is black" (Sloan, 1963). The success of a firm during that period was based on having the lowest price. In the next phase, changes in the environment caused changes in the behavior and approach of companies. There was an incremental change in the boundaries of the environment that led to unexpected challenges. It was the age of discontinuity, according to Peter Drucker (1969).

The model of a successful company, and its behavior, is of interest to researchers. Through the years, several researchers have analyzed the concepts of environment, strategy and capability, but only a few have examined their relationship and interdependence. These researchers could be classified into two groups—dynamic and static—depending on the way they analyzed or perceived these attributes.

The dynamic researchers were those who studied the evolution of an organization and its behavior over a period of time. They found that organizations react to certain political and socio-economic signals from the environment. Chandler (1962) was the first to present this behavior of firms, focusing his attention on how strategy and structure respond in the perspective of time.

On the other hand, the static researchers examined the behavior of organizations at a certain point in time, trying to identify the organization's success model by correlating among the variables which led to success. Ansoff (1987) presented the models of strategic behavior representing four theoretical viewpoints proposed by the dynamic researchers (see Figure 6.2).

| Model of Success | Change in Process: | |
	Incremental	Discontinuous
Organic	March & Simon	
Reactive	J. Thompson	A. Chandler
Ad Hoc	B. Quinn	H. Mintzberg
Systematic	G. Steiner	H. I. Ansoff

**Figure 6.2: Dynamic Researchers' Models of
            Strategic Behavior**

DYNAMIC RESEARCHERS

March and Simon (1958) directed attention into the organization, and especially to the human element. They examined the organic part as having a direct overall influence, together with the relationship between member groups, conflicts and how conflicts can be resolved. The organizational structure was considered as consisting of aspects of behavior which are reasonably stable when changes in the environment occur. March and Simon also connected innovation with the level of aspiration of the individual, where both are affected by the environment.

The success model of Cyert and March (1963) was based on the following three moving lines of development:

1. sociological,
2 psycho-sociological, and
3. administrative.

Their theory focused on the administrative process of decision-making as affected by the sociological and psycho-sociological aspects. Planning, as the main element of decision-making, was used to reduce environmental uncertainty.

Thompson (1967) tried to find out what made organizations act and how they acted. He dealt with the organization as a system, and his attention was focused on the openness and closedness of the system where certain strategies applied. Thompson suggested that the crucial problems in the assessment of a company position were how an organization knows when it has maximized achievement, and how it assesses its fitness for the future.

The dynamic researchers dealt with structure according to the openness and closedness of the system, depending on the individual members. The decision-making process was presented as a matrix of cause and effect and certainty-uncertainty dimensions (Bourgois, 1980; Duncan, 1972).

Chandler (1962) in a historical description of companies, recognized the importance of environmental turbulence. According to Chandler, an incrementally discontinuous environment exists before a survival crisis strikes and a new strategy is implemented to produce satisfactory financial performance.

Chandler showed that there was a mismatch of strategy and the structural configuration necessary for success in the changed environment. As a result, there is a period of adaptation where strategy and structure evolve, and eventually again come into balance.

Henry Mintzberg (1973, 1979) examined organizational design, groups, decision making, power of members, the span of control, and introduced the concept of ad hoc management. He then developed his hypothesis about the relationship between environment and structure: "The more complex the environment, the more decentralized the structure." Environment and structure were put in a matrix where environment was classified as stable, dynamic, complex and simple; structure was classifed as centralized, decentralized, organic and bureaucratic.

Researchers such as Steiner (1969, 1981), and Ansoff (1965, 1984), saw the organization as guided by a more comprehensive preplanned strategy. In their model, comprehensively managed firms try to anticipate, rather than to react to, an upcoming crisis. Strategic decisions are made by thorough analysis of environment, structure, capability and performance.

Ansoff (1978) recognized the importance of environment and extensively analyzed the concept as an influence on the decision of strategic behavior of a firm. According to Ansoff, the environment pressures the company to use its resources effectively in anticipation of changes in that environment. The firm is under pressure to perform because lack of performance would lead to failure to survive. Ansoff described the phenomenon as an interaction of survival drive, organization inertia, strategic leadership, culture, aggressiveness and capability.

The conjunction of survival and performance, and the rational model, led Ansoff to the development of the model of strategic behavior of a firm, which makes possible an analysis of the relationship between the firm's environment, strategy, capability and performance.

STATIC RESEARCHERS

The second group is the static researchers who analyzed the behavior of a firm at a given point in time, trying to identify the relationship of variables of strategic behavior to the success of the firm.

Chandler (1962) made a historical presentation of events through the years, and identified stages of environmental discontinuity leading to strategic adaptation and balance between strategy and structure. He examined structure as the combination of organizational structure, systems and planning.

Rummelt (1974) examined the behavior of firms belonging in the *Fortune* 500 for the years 1949, 1959 and 1969. He identified company diversification of growth as a strategy for success. Structure, according to Rummelt, was examined more as the organogram of the organization, even though he states that structure consists of "systems of control, planning, information flow, methods of reward and punishment, and degree of delegation."

Channon (1973) focused his attention on the sequence of strategy and structure in order to achieve normative performance. In concluding a survey on British enterprises, he wrote:

> *The adoption of the new strategy (triggered by the changes of the environment) also brought a dramatic change in the administrative structure of the large corporate enterprise. The multi-divisional structure provided the administrative mechanism to control, consolidate and institutionalize the new strategy.* (p. 238)

Thorelli (1977) discussed the issues of strategy, structure and performance. He differentiated between the environment inside and outside of the company and/or bargaining power. Thorelli talked about performance, but he did not say how the performance was affected when changes of strategy and structure occur. Steiner (1981, 1983) stressed the importance of strategy as the factor affecting a firm's performance.

Modern organizations exist in turbulent, often hostile, environments which pose constant threats to their growth and survival. Steers (1977) summarized the importance of the environment:

> *The capacity of an organization to successfully adapt to its environment is facilitated to a large extent by its ability to know what the external environment is going to be like in the future.* (p. 96)

One important dimension is the degree of environmental instability. Emery and Trist (1965) discussed the concept of turbulence, its complexity and instability. They developed four steps of the texturing of the environment described through two case studies. According to Ansoff (1979, 1984, 1990), the turbulence of the environment consists of five levels of turbulence, influenced by the elements of discontinuity and changeability of the environment.

Ansoff (1965) was an early researcher of this theme. He suggested and defined the concept of turbulence as a measure of the change that occurs in the factors or components of an organization's environment.

According to Ansoff (1965), the level of turbulence is the state of knowledge at which environment-serving organizations in the industry must start reacting in order to respond effectively to environmental changes. At one end of a continuum of change there is a static/stable/repetitive environmental state (no change); at the other end, a turbulent or dynamic/surpriseful state where all factors are in constant flux. The amount of turbulence is closely related to the degree of uncertainty facing a firm. As the environment becomes increasingly turbulent, factors become less predictable and more uncertain, and the values of important variables themselves move in an erratic fashion.

Jurkovitch (1974) suggested that the rate of change of the environment can be identified by measuring the amount of changes and alternatives to major goals in a given period. He found that the higher the change rate of the environment, the higher the number of major organizational goals that must be altered and vice versa.

While Ansoff (1984, 1990) gives a complete overview of 1) the levels of turbulence of the environments, 2) the elements which influence each of the levels, and 3) the signals of changes in the levels of the environment, Emery and Trist (1965) talked only about the levels of turbulence, and Jurkovitch (1974) examined only the signals of changeability of the environment.

Ansoff (1984, 1990) operationalized the level of turbulence of the environment from closed to open, or stable to surpriseful, where different solutions apply to different levels of turbulence when appropriate.

The second major subdimension of the external environment is that of discontinuity. This dimension is concerned with the number of environmental factors that must be considered by the firm in a decision-making process.

In a simple environment, an organization does not need sophisticated information systems since only a limited number of information categories are critical for organizational decision-making to be monitored. Complex environments, in contrast, place greater demands on an information system and call for a higher quality of decision-making to respond to diverse environmental constituencies.

The concept of environmental turbulence has been closely intertwined with the need for strategy reformulation. A number of authors (Chandler, 1962; Miles, Snow and Pfeffer, 1974; Ansoff, 1979; Camillus, 1982), have contended that as turbulence increases, the impetus for formulation of a new strategy increases. An empirical study by Lindsay and Rue (1978) found support for the proposition that the level of perceived environmental turbulence did affect the planning process and the resulting strategy.

A matrix representing the impact of the external environment of organizations is shown in Figure 6.3.

Environment	Response on Organization
Incremental Change	Incremental response of the organization 1.1 If there is myopia ➡ Crisis 1.2 If development unpredictable ➡ Crisis 2 If there is anticipation ➡ Timely Discontinuous Response

Figure 6.3: Impact of Environment on Organizations

Lenz and Engledow (1986) identified five approaches to modeling the environment, varying in their assumptions about the structure of the environment, problems, and causes of change, as well as in assumptions about how researchers analyze the turbulence of the environment. The environment should be viewed as acting directly on the strategic behavior of the firms through strategic choice (Ansoff, 1984; Child, 1972). Or, the impact of the environment on a firm's strategic behavior should conform to propositions on perceived changeability and discontinuity (Rhyne, 1985). Jauch, Osborn and Glueck (1980) examined the interaction effects of the changes of the environment and strategic behavior, and found that these were not significant. On the other hand, Hitt, Ireland and Standler (1982), in examining separately the effects of environment and strategy on performance, found significant moderating effects on the relationships of the variables. The impact of environmental turbulence on a firm's strategic behavior was expected to conform to the following propositions, modified from Rhyne (1985, p. 323):

1. The greater the perceived discontinuity of an organization's environment, the more sophisticated its planning system.

2. The greater the perceived changeability of an organization's environment, the more sophisticated its planning system.

Cyert (1973) summarized the issue of organization and environment in the following paragraph:

The organization and the environment are part of a complex interactive system. The actions taken by the organization can have important effects on the environment and conversely, the outcomes of the actions of the organizations are partially those determined by events in the environment. Those outcomes and events that contribute to them have a major impact on the organization. Even if the organization does not respond to these events, significant changes in the organizational participant's goal and roles can occur. (p. 352)

STRATEGIC BEHAVIOR

Strategic behavior is the behavior of the firm's strategy influenced by:

1. the decision-making rules for guidance of organizational behavior, according to Ansoff (1984, p. 31), and

2. the aggressiveness of the firm's strategy.

The firm develops a certain strategy consisting of decision-making rules concerning the firm's objectives, its external and internal behavior, and its operating policy. The strategic behavior consists of the configuration of these rules in conjunction with the aggressiveness of the firm's strategy. The changeability of the environment is embodied in the strategic behavior of a firm through the aggressiveness of the firm's strategy.

Strategic behavior has long been identified as an essential function of management. Many writers point out that the problem is not with the fundamental utility of strategic behavior, but with the nature of the planning systems (Higgins, 1981; Peters, 1982; Peters and Waterman, 1982; Peters, 1987). As actually implemented, many planning systems bear little resemblance to the process described in strategic management literature. In an appraisal of current planning in the United States, Steiner (1983) concluded that clear identification of purposes of strategic planning and strategic thinking were two areas in which actual planning systems fell short of the ideal.

A major reason for the failure of firms to conduct true strategic planning appears to be related to a lack of appropriate information to facilitate that process. The importance of relevant information to strategy formulation has frequently been emphasized in the literature. In addition, a number of authors have described specific systems to provide information (King and Cleland, 1974; King, Dutta and Rodriguez, 1978; Radford, 1978; King and Rodriguez, 1981; Grant and King,

1982). Other authors have presented techniques by which executives can break down preconceived patterns of thought to identify the information necessary to support their strategic decision-making (Mitroff and Emshoff, 1979; Cosier, 1981).

Strategic management theory holds that the fundamental goal of planning is to produce a strategy which achieves a match, fit or alignment of internal resources and capabilities with external opportunities and threats. Others have argued that strategy formulation primarily takes place on an informal basis and is not necessarily communicated to the organization as a whole. Camillus (1982) labelled the first position as synoptic formalism and the second as logical incrementalism, and concluded that both approaches have an appropriate role. Extensive analysis leading to a major shift in strategy can and should take place frequently. The intervening period could be used to refine strategy execution. However, some means of monitoring the environment between the synoptic formalism exercises would be required to ensure that the assumptions upon which the strategy was based remained valid.

Rhyne (1985) presents a definable difference between long range planning and strategic planning as follows:

> *Regardless of the process by which it takes place, the analysis/adaptive (openness) dimension must be addressed, for true strategic planning is qualitatively different from long-range planning. In strategic planning the firm's dominion remains open to investigation and redefinition. Long-range planning assumes the firm's domain to be essentially given. (p. 319-337)*

The contribution of Ansoff (1984) is on the overall input of strategic management and the influence of the organization. Technology and information are contained within a term called the "aggressiveness" of the strategic behavior of the firm. Agressiveness is defined as follows:

> *Strategic aggressiveness is the degree of discontinuity which a firm introduces into succeeding generations of its products, technologies and marketing concepts. It describes a class of competitive strategies which have the same behavioral aggressiveness.*

The strategic aggressiveness identifies the level of discontinuity and allows the development of the desired strategy for optimal performance.

Ansoff (1979) held that the degree to which an organization is successful in integrating such information into its planning will determine the level of strategic thrust of that organization.

CAPABILITY

The concept of capability is relatively new. For a long time, writers were dealing with one element of capability at a time. Some writers thought capability was only the organizational structure of a company. Burns and Stalker (1961), Etzioni (1964), Thompson (1967), Silverman (1970) and Galbraith (1973) analyzed and discussed the relationship and influence of organizational structure on the effective operation of organizations.

The human element is also important. Cyert and March (1963), Argyris (1964), Blake and Mouton (1964), Likert (1967), Bersberg (1968) and Schein (1970) talked about the integration of the individual with the organization. Steiner (1977, 1979) directed the attention towards the issue of planning. According to Steiner, planning was considered the main element of the successful organization. It was related to environment and strategy. Planning, according to Steiner (1979), is the human responsibility of all managers. He defines strategic planning as being a process of formal structure, a way of life and the futurity of current events.

The issue of corporate culture surfaced as one of the elements that makes organizations more efficient. Deal and Kennedy (1982) present an in-depth analysis of the elements of corporate culture and how they can be applied and used in the organization affectively.

BUSINESS CULTURE

Corporate culture is viewed from two perspectives: (1) from a cultural/social standpoint, and (2) from a business standpoint (see Figure 6.4). Edgar Schein (1983) defined culture as follows:

> *Culture is the pattern of basic assumptions that a given group has invented, discovered, or developed in learning to cope with its problems of external adaptation and internal integration—a pattern of assumptions that has worked well enough to be considered valid, and therefore, to be taught to new members as the correct way to perceive, think and feel in relation to those problems. (p. 13-25)*

CORPORATE CULTURE

Wheelen and Hunger (1983) defined culture as the collection of beliefs, expectations and values shared by the corporation's members and transmitted from one generation of employees to another.

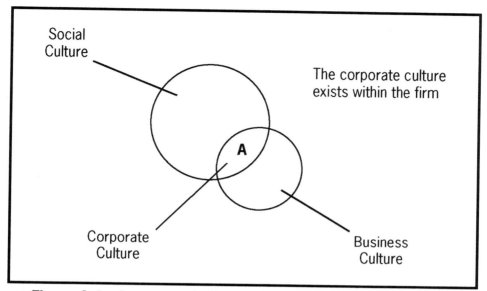

Figure 6.4: Corporate Culture

A definition presenting an overview on culture was proposed by Pettigrew (1979), who said that culture is the system of such publicly and collectively accepted meanings operating from a given group at a given time.

From a business point of view, Siehl and Martin (1981) and Tichy (1982) defined corporate culture as "social and normative glue that holds an organization together"—shown as area A in Figure 6.4. Corporate culture expresses the values, or social ideals, and the beliefs that organization members come to share.

From the social point of view, Spradley and McCurdy (1975) defined culture as "the acquired knowledge people use to interpret experience and generate social behavior." Werner and Topper (1979) defined culture as "the system of knowledge that explains the social and physical universe and provides plans and decisions for coping." Harris and Moran (1979) defined culture as "the communicable knowledge for human coping within a particular environment that is passed on for the benefit of subsequent generations." Their anthropological point of view is pertinent to the present study because it identifies and defines the grounds/boundaries where the business profile develops.

Corporate strategic profile develops in accordance with the environment contributing to the internal integration of the firm. It specifies the boundaries within which the firm behaves in the external environment. As an extension of the model proposed by Fombrun (1983), the external environment consists of the following:

1. The industrial environment—
    • Competitors in the similar industry, technology.

2. The societal environment—
    • Political, social, legal, at a local level in the city/area in which the firm functions.

3. The national environment—
    • Economic, social, legal, political, as part of the country.

4. The international environment—
    • The environment out of national limits of the country. The firm is exposed to international regulations, customs, tariffs, quotas and the specific environment of the country with which the firm is dealing.

In the literature on capability, there has been a transition from considering individual elements of capability to the view which holds that all of the elements of capability are essential to success. Peter Drucker (1974, 1979) attempted a configuration of the elements of capability, but ended by concentrating on the management by objective issue, one of the elements of capability. Harold Leavitt (1964) talked about the systematic interrelationship of the elements of capability and illustrated an integration of the elements of capability, as shown in Figure 6.5.

While Leavitt (1964, 1975) developed a conceptual integrative presentation of the elements of capability, Ansoff (1984) operationalized them into systems, structures, culture, etc. Ansoff (1978, 1984) defined and operationalized the concept of capability. Following Leavitt, Ansoff suggested that capability consists of two parts: the human and the systems. The human part is the mentality, power, talent, corporate culture, skills and knowledge; in other words, the software of the operation. The systems are the organizational structure, systems, information and technological assistance. The systems are the hardware of the operation.

Ansoff's contribution on the issue of capability includes the following points:

1. The components of capability are mutually important and all have to be in tune for the organization to be efficient.

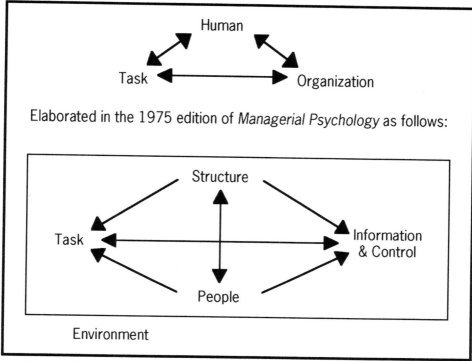

Figure 6.5: Elements of Capability

2. At different times, different elements of capability become more critical, depending on the level of discontinuity.

3. At different levels of turbulence, the demand for success requires different capability profiles.

See Figure 6.6 for Ansoff's (1984, p. 209) presentation of the elements of general management capability.

SUPPORTING STUDIES

Eight additional studies have analyzed the applicability of the success hypothesis and tested the study reported herein. These studies took place after the completion of this primary study and reinforce its validity.

Salameh (1987) examined the strategic behavior of the banking industry in the United Arab Emirates. He interviewed 51 percent of the top managers of UAE,

	Managers	Organization
Climate (Will to Respond)	mentality power position	culture power structure
Competence (Ability to Respond)	talents skills	structures systems
Capacity (Volume of Response)	personal	organizational

Figure 6.6: General Management Capability

who also represented 71 percent of the total Abu Dhabi banks. In his study, Salameh examined the relationship between environment, strategy, capability, and performance. He found that smaller strategic gaps were accompanied by better financial performance (see Figure 6.7). He also stressed that outside observers are excellent sources of strategic information regarding the environment.

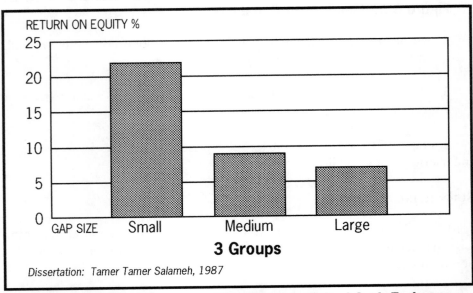

Dissertation: *Tamer Tamer Salameh, 1987*

**Figure 6.7: Performance of 25 Banks in United Arab Emirates
         vs. Strategic Gap**

Sullivan (1987) also dealt with the success hypothesis for public entities. Sixty-nine Federal agencies analyzed in his study were competing under the commercial activity program. Sullivan found that agencies or organizations that were more dependent on transaction income from the business environment were more adaptable to environmental change. These agencies also exhibited better strategic behavior and strategic performance. Agencies or organizations that had a strategic thrust matching the level of environmental turbulence and strategic capability exhibited better strategic performance (see Figure 6.8).

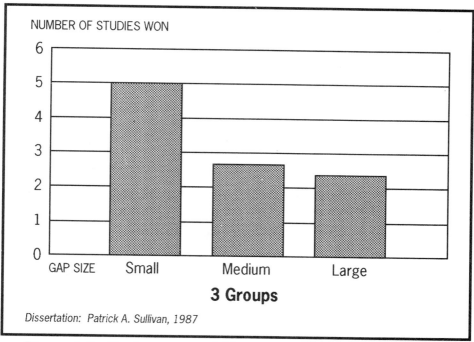

NUMBER OF STUDIES WON

GAP SIZE — Small — Medium — Large

3 Groups

Dissertation: Patrick A. Sullivan, 1987

Figure 6.8: Performance of 69 U.S. Federal Agency Public Works Organizations vs. Strategic Gap

Chabane (1987) examined the success hypothesis for Algerian state-owned enterprises. Thirty-four Algerian manufacturing companies were analyzed in his study. He found that because of the challenge of the business environment, state-owned enterprises shifted from social status to efficiency status, focusing and responding to calls of the environment (see Figure 6.9).

Lewis (1989) examined the strategic posture and financial performance of the banking industry in California. He analyzed 22 banks representing 105 branches in

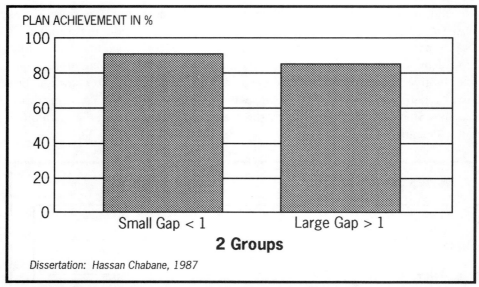

**Figure 6.9: Performance of 34 Algerian State-Owned
Enterprises vs. Strategic Gap**

San Diego County. He found that banks which did not perceive environmental turbulence correctly did not perform as well as those that did. A low strategy-capability gap resulted in increased profit potential for the bank. Optimum financial performance occurred when the levels of environmental turbulence, aggressiveness of strategy, and general management capability were aligned. Decreases of any of the gaps contributed to better financial performance. Companies with .5 gap between the variables had better financial performance than those with 1.5 gap. If there was more than a 1.5 gap, there was negative performance. Three companies went bankrupt during his study; all three firms had gap levels of more than 1.5.

Jaja (1990) also examined the success hypothesis, emphasizing the implications of technological change on the financial performance of commercial banks. He analyzed 35 large commercial banks in the United States. He found that commercial banks with more narrow perceptions of how technologies can be used to exploit market opportunities in the business environment are in danger of losing their competitive positioning because they are unprofitable. He also found that the financial performance of commercial banks is directly related to the size of the gap between technological turbulence and the business environment of banking. Additionally, he found that the commercial banks that reported smaller gaps in the technology strategic posture performed better than banks with larger gaps. He found that when organizational capability transformation is first installed, followed by a change of strategic posture, first, there is adjustment to the capability change and second, to the strategy.

Wang (1991) examined the strategic gap and management capability of U.S. savings and loan associations. He analyzed 39 savings and loan associations and found that the financial performance was inversely related to the strategic gap. Companies with a gap between environment, strategy and management capability were poor performers. In particular, two of the S&Ls analyzed went bankrupt during the study; these were the worst performers of the group. Since then, more of the financial institutions found to have a gap went bankrupt.

Djohar (1991) completed a study of 97 Indonesian manufacturing firms. He looked for a strategic gap between environment, strategy and capability, and tested the strategic success hypothesis, finding that companies with no gap performed better than ones with a gap between the above independent variables. He also found a direct correlation between strategic efficiency and competitive efficiency affecting the companies' profit potential.

Mitiku (1991) also completed a study on state-owned enterprised in Ethiopia. He analyzed 54 companies, testing the strategic success hypothesis, and found that companies without a gap between the strategic variables performed better than those with a gap. His findings were based on using the ratio *return on assets* as a dependent variable.

The above eight studies support the strategic success hypothesis in a variety of business environments. A total of 431 companies were analyzed with consistent results. There were 210 U.S.-based manufacturers; wholesale, retail and government agencies; and banks and financial institutions. There were 221 international manufacturers, state-owned enterprises, banks and financial institutions.

These eight supporting studies took place within a five-year period, with the same focus and the same strategic success hypothesis. The findings in all 431 cases supported the conclusion that companies without a gap between environment, strategy and capability outperformed companies with a gap.

Chapter 7
CONCLUSION

These nine studies illustrate the need for a company to be constantly aware of its position *vis-a-vis* its environment in order for it to remain financially successful.

All companies develop strategies in order to maintain or improve their competitive position in their industry by answering the following questions:

1. What business are we in?

2. Where are we now?

3. Where do we want to be?

4. How do we get there?

The firm must evaluate its external environment with an eye toward identifying potential opportunities and threats, in order to be in a position to act rather than react. In an effort to remain competitive, the manager must clearly see the firm in relation to its rivals. After having identified and clarified environmental forces and trends affecting the company, the manager is positioned to build strategies to ensure financial success. This master strategy is supported by the business strategies for each SBA, which in turn are supported by the functional strategies of each department. To assist managers in any, or all, of the steps in the development of strategy, this study found that Ansoff's instrument is a valuable functional tool. This instrument analyzes the forces of the external environment and assists in the analysis of a company's internal position. It addresses the support functions within the company that are necessary to efficiently implement the strategy and ensure that the desired results are achieved.

The results of this study illustrate that companies which are environmentally aware of changes within their industry, and utilize innovation as a tool for corrective action, are more financially successful than those that are unable to respond to the changing nature of their environment.

Appendix A
THE INSTRUMENT *

Strategic Posture Analysis Exercise: Procedure A-1

Matching Environment, Strategy, and General Management Capability

The purposes of this procedure are to:

I.   Choose strategic business area and time span of analysis.

II. Assess the turbulence of the firm's environment.

III. Determine changes needed in the aggressiveness of the firm's strategy.

IV. Determine the change in the general management capability needed to support the new strategy.

V.   Establish program priorities.

VI. Establish a program for change.

VII. Define measures to assure effective implementation of transformation.

---

* Adapted from October 1990 revision of the instrument by H. Igor Ansoff and Denny Soinski to make it easier to use; the revision also shifts emphasis from *detecting* gaps to *correcting* any identified gaps.

I. Choice of Strategic Business Area and Time Span of Analysis

1. Enter the name of the firm: _____
2. Select and enter the name of the unit of the firm you want to analyze (name of a division, a strategic business unit, etc.): _____
3. Select and enter the name of a segment of the chosen unit's environment (a strategic business area or a major market segment): _____
4. Identify the time span for which you will focus your analysis:

   i. Enter T_1, the number of years it normally takes to develop and launch a new generation product line in the strategic business area you have selected.
   ii. Enter T_2 the total number of years from now until the new product line will have to be divested.
   iii. Take the difference $(T_2 - T_1)$ and enter below:
   $$T_1 = \underline{\hspace{1cm}} \text{ years} \qquad T_2 = \underline{\hspace{1cm}} \text{ years}$$
   $$\text{Time Span} = T_2 - T_1 = \underline{\hspace{1cm}} \text{ years}$$

II. Future Level of Environmental Turbulence

1. In Figure A-1, construct a profile of the marketing turbulence in the environment as it will likely be during the future time span. Do this by circling the relevant columns for each attribute in Table A-1.

2. Examine the resulting zig-zag profile formed by the circled entries and draw two vertical lines for marketing turbulence on Figure A-3 which best describe the range of profitable response in the marketing environment. (Firms which respond as if turbulence were below this range would be lagging behind the environment and probably would be unprofitable. Firms which respond as if turbulence were higher than this range would be "outrunning" the environment and also would be unprofitable.)

3. Repeat the process for the range of profitable response in the innovation environment, using Table A-2, by drawing two corresponding vertical lines.

4. Using the results of the above steps, mark the ranges of the profitable marketing and innovation responses on the corresponding scales of Figure A-3.

III. Aggressiveness of Firm's Strategy

1. Using TableA-4, identify the aggressiveness of the firm's present innovation strategy. To do this, first circle applicable characteristics as above, and then draw an average single vertical line through the table which best describes the aggressiveness of the firm's innovation strategy.

2. Enter this line on the scale "innovation strategy" on Figure A-3 to represent the firm's present innovation strategy.

3. Repeat steps 1 and 2 for the marketing strategy of the firm, using Table A-5 and entering this line on the appropriate scale of Figure A-3.

4. Select the strategies which the company's Environment Serving Organization (ESO) should develop for the time span period. Enter this in Figure A-3 by marking points for innovation strategy and marketing strategy on the appropriate scales. Both points should fall inside the range of strategies needed for profitable response, but their exact position should be based on judgments about the following points:

    i. Objectives for the ESO in the SBA.
    ii. Aggressiveness of the SBU management.
    iii. Commonality of present and selected strategies.
    iv. Applicability of the firm's present capabiities to selected strategies.

    (For example, firms strong in production would choose strategies near the lower level of marketing turbulence and of innovation turbulence; firms strong in marketing would choose a strategy near the higher level of marketing turbulence, and companies strong in R & D would choose a strategy near the higher level in the innovation environment.

5. Take into consideration:

    i. the time, T_1, normally needed to develop a new product/process line, and

    ii. the likely aggressiveness of the competitors in the SBA, estimates of the time available, T_3, within which the firm must implement the respective strategies if it wants to become one of the top competitors in the SBA.

Estimate and enter at the top of Figure A-7 the target time duration for transformation of the strategies.

IV. Capability to Support Strategy

1. Turning attention inside the firm, determine the present profile of the firm's general management capability. Do this by circling the characteristics which best describe the firm for each of the capability components in Figure A-6. Construct a profile, and for each component, draw a vertical line which best describes the component. (The components are: culture, managers, structure, systems, management technology and management capacity.)

2. Enter these averages on the appropriate lines of Figure A-3 and construct the present capability profile by joining the entries by line segments. Label it C_1.

3. Examine the marketing strategy and innovation strategy ranges and decide on the capability, C_2, which the firm should develop. (To support the strategy fully, C_2 must be matched to the more aggressive strategy. However, you may decide on a compromise, or you may want to have a higher level of capability than dictated by S_2 in order to anticipate further increases in environmental turbulence beyond the time span of your analysis.) Draw a vertical line on Figure A-3 for the desired capability profile and label it C_2. Also draw the C_2 line on each page of Figure A-6.

4. Compare C_1 and C_2 and estimate the target number of years for development of the new general management capability of the SBU.

    The estimate should be based on:

    i.   The size of the capability gaps.
    ii. The long development lead time components (such as culture).
    iii. The target number of years you have chosen for strategy development.
    iv. The total resources per year which the firm can devote to both strategy and capability development.

    Since components of capability, such as culture, require long development time, you may have to choose a longer capability development period than the target period you have chosen for the strategies.

On the other hand, a shorter target period for development of capability will contribute to the efficiency of the strategy implementation process.

Enter the estimate at the top of Figure A-7.

V. Priorities for Organizational Change

1. In Figure A-3, measure the gaps between the present strategies and future strategies, and present and future capability components (round off the size of the gaps to the nearest one-half). Enter the gaps into Figure A-7.

2. Assign priorities to the programs shown in Column 3 of Figure A-7 (to help you choose priorities for the capability programs, refer to Figure A-6). Use 1 for highest priority and 10 for lowest. Enter the priorities into Figure A-7.

3. If only three characteristics (among the 24) were to be chosen for immediate improvements, which ones would you choose? Circle these in Table A-6.

VI. Program for Change

1. Under "other" in the first column of Figure A-7, write names of programs which you may feel are necessary in addition to the ones listed, and assign gaps and priorities to them.

2. Since both strategy and capability changes will place heavy demands on the firm's resources, it is necessary to budget for them. Make estimates of the costs of 1) formulating and implementing the new strategies and 2) transforming the general management capabilities. Enter the costs in Figure A-7.

3. Taking account of the priorities, distribute initial and final year's budgets among the programs. Enter results in columns 4 and 5 in Figure A-7.

4. Using the priorities, construct in Figure A-8 a Gantt chart of the organizational transformation; next to each program draw a horizontal line starting at the year of initiation and stopping at the year of termination.

VII. Measures to Assure Effective Implementation of the Transformation

1. If the time needed for the transformation is less than the time available (see Part III, section 5), you should not expect any difficulties in completing the transformation on time. However, you may encounter problems and challenges in the course of the transformation (such as resistance to change, lack of resources, etc.). Identify such problems and/or challenges and enter these in the left-hand column of Figure A-9.

2. If the time needed exceeds the time available, you may encounter additional problems. Identify these in the left-hand column of Figure A-9.

3. In the middle column of Figure A-9, describe what action should be taken to deal with each problem.

4. In the right-hand column, identify who (person or organizational unit) should be responsible for anticipating and solving each problem.

Attr.	Level of Turbulence	Reactive	Expanding	Changing	Discontinuous	Surpriseful
1.	% of Industry Profit Spent on Marketing	Low (5% or less)	Low	Moderate	High	Very High (30% or more)
2.	Market Structure	Monopoly	Oligopoly	Oligopoly	Multi-competitor	Major New Entrants
3.	Aggressiveness of Leading Competitors	Low	Defensive	Aggressive	Very Aggressive	Very Aggressive
4.	Pressure by Customers	None	Weak	Strong	Demanding	Threatening
5.	$\underline{DEMAND} = D$ Industry Capacity	$D>>1$	$D>1$	$D=1$	$D<1$	$D<<1$
6.	Stage in Industry Life Cycle	Maturity-Decline	Early Growth	Late Growth	Late Growth, Emergence, or Decline	Shift in Stage, Emergence, or Decline
7.	Profitability	High	High	Moderate	Low	Low
8.	Product Differentiation	None	Low	Moderate-High	—	—
9.	Critical Marketing Success Factors	Control of Market	Dominant Market Share / Low Production Cost	Product Appeal / Response to Customer Needs	Anticipation of Changes / Responsiveness to Changing Customer Values	Identification of latent needs

Figure A-1: Levels of Marketing Turbulence

Attr.	Level of Turbulence	Reactive	Expanding	Changing	Discontinuous	Surpriseful
1.	% of Industry Sales Spent on R & D	Low (5% or less)	Low	Moderate	High	Very High (50% or more)
2.	Frequency of New Product in Industry	Infrequent (every 5 or more years)	Low	Moderate	High	High (several/year)
3.	Length of Product Life Cycle	Long (5 yrs. or longer)	Long	Moderate	Short	Short (less than 1 yr.)
4.	Rate of Change of Technology	Very Slow	Slow	Fast-Moderate	Influx of Foreign Technols.	Emergence of Novel Technols.
5.	Diversity of Competing Technologies	None	None	None	Several	Several
6.	State of Industry Life Cycle	Maturity	Early Growth	Late Growth	Emergence of Decline	Emergence, Decline or Shift in Stage
7.	Profitability	High	High	Moderate	Low	Low
8.	Critical Innovation Success Factors	Cost-Reduction	Product Adaptation	Product Improvement	Product Innovation	Creativity

Figure A-2: Levels of Innovation Turbulence

	Stable	Reactive	Anticipating	Exploring	Creative
Marketing Turbulence (E^M)					
Marketing Strategy (S^M)					
Innovation Turbulence (E^I)					
Innovation Strategy (S^I)					
Capability (C):					
Culture					
Manager					
Structure					
Systems					
Technology					
Capacity					
	1	2	3	4	5

Figure A-3: Balance Between Environment, Strategy and Capability

Attr.	Level of Turbulence	Stable	Reactive	Anticipatory	Exploratory	Creative
1.	Responsiveness to Customers	Neglect	"Our Product is what the Customer Wants"	Anticipation of Needs	Identification of Unfilled Needs	Identification of Latent Needs
2.	Focus of Product Development	Process Efficiency & Product Durability	Product Imitation & Product Cost Reduction	Rounding Out of Product & Product Improvement	Product Innovation	Product Pioneering Line
3.	Market Development	"Stick to Our Customers"	"Follow Competitors"	Expand to Familiar Markets	Expand to Foreign Markets	Create New Markets
4.	Focus of Research	None	Technology Imitation	Technology Improvement	Adaptation of Novel Technology	Pioneering New Technologies
5.	Frequency of New Product Introduction	Rare (every 5 or more years)	Low	Moderate	High	High (several per year)
6.	% of Sales in R & D	Low	Low	Moderate	High	Very High
7.	Role of R & D Department	"Seen but not Heard"	"Called in When When Necessary"	Support of Marketing	Source of New Products	"The Elite"
8.	Responsibility for Innovation	Not Identified	Functionally Divided Between R & D and Marketing		Assigned to New Product/ New Venture Department	

Figure A-4: Aggressiveness of Firm's Innovation Strategy

Attr.	Level of Turbulence	Stable	Reactive	Anticipatory	Exploratory	Creative
1.	Sales Aggressiveness	Low	Moderate	High	Very High	Very High
2.	Responsiveness to Competition	"We Do Not Compete"	"We Will Respond to Aggression"	"We Will Not Be Undersold"	"We Lead The Pack"	"We Are Our Own Competitors"
3.	Market Share	"Growth With Market"	Defend	Increase	Control	Dominate
4.	Promotion/ Advertising	"Our Products Speak for Themselves"	Reactive	Aggressive	Advanced	Creative
5.	Marketing	None	Traditional	Advanced	Innovative	Creative
6.	Percentage of Firms' Sales in Marketing	Very Low (< 5%)				Very High (> 30%)
7.	Role of Marketing Department	"To Sell What the Firm Produces"	"To Convince Customers Our Products Are Superior"	"To Serve the Customers"	"To Establish the Firm as a Marketing Leader"	"To Establish the Firm as a Marketing Innovator"

Figure A-5: Aggressiveness of Firm's Marketing Strategy

Component	Custodial	Production	Marketing	Strategic	Flexible
Culture					
1. Rewards and Incentives	Length of Service	Past Performance	Contribution to Future Growth	Entrepreneurship	Creativity
2. Values and Attitudes	Don't Rock the Boat	Roll with the Punches	Grow!	Diversify!	Create the Future!
3. Attitude Toward Change	Reject	React	Seek Familiar Change	Seek Novel Change	Create Change
4. Success Criterion	Stability	Efficient Performance	Response to Competition and Market Needs	Dynamic Balance of SBA Portfolio	Leadership Through Innovation
Managers					
5. Leadership Style	Political/ Custodial	Diciplinary/ Controllership	Inspirational/ Common Purpose	Charismatic	Visionary
6. Problem Solving	Trial and Error	Diagnostic	Optimization	Seek Alternatives	Creative
7. Risk Propensity	Reject	Accept Familiar Risk	Seek Familiar Risk	Seek Novel Risk	Gamble on Innovation
8. Knowledge	Internal Politics	Internal Operations	Traditional Markets	Global Environment	Emerging Environment
9. Perception of Success Factors	• Stability • Repetition	• Growth • Economies of Scale • Lowest Price	• Response to Market Needs • Competitive Differentiation	• Strat. Positioning • Balanced Portfolio • Flexibility • Societal Responsiveness	• Technological Activity • Needs Creativity

Structure

10. Organizational Form	Bureaucratic	Functional	Divisional	New Ventures/Matrix	Flexible
11. Job Definition	Specific Task	Performance Area	Growth Area	Field of Opportunity	Field of Creativity
12. Org. Flexibility	Rigid	Low	Moderate	Adaptive	Highly Adaptive
13. Power Structure	Many Centers	Centralized	Decentralized	Bicentralized	Centralized
14. Power Center	Bureaucracy	Production	Marketing	General Mgmt.	R & D

Systems

15. Informal Decision	Very Slow/Hierarchy-centered	Slow/Function-centered	Moderately Fast/Division-centered	Fast/Matrix-centered	Very Fast/Problem-centered
16. Information	Precedent-based	Historical Performance	Extrapolated Future	New Futures	Potential Futures
17. Problem Priorities	Power Struggle	Performance	Growth	New Opportunities	Creativity
18. Problem Trigger	React to Crisis Crisis	Accumulation of Unsatisfactory Performance	Anticipated Threats	New Opportunities	Breakthroughs
19. Decision System	Systems and Procedures	Budgeting	Long-range planning	Strategic Planning Management	Strategic Issue Management Crisis Mgmt.

Figure A-6: Management Capability Profile

Component	Custodial	Production	Marketing	Strategic	Flexible
Systems cont.					
20. Control Signal	Deviation from Stable State	Deviation from Budgets	Deviation From Plans	Shortage of Opportunities	Loss of Creativity
21. Implementation	Directive/ by Exception	Directive/ Regular	Consultative/ Regular	Consultative/ by Exception	Consultative/ by Exception
Management Technology					
22. Analytic Models	Standardized Procedures	Work Study/ Ratio Analysis/ Equipment Replacement	Capital Budgeting Optimization	Futurology	Creativity
23. Computer Applications	Statistical Files	Statistical Performance Control	Performance Extrapolation	Non-linear Forecasting What-if-models	Artifical Intelligence
Management Capacity					
24. General Mgmt.	Minimal				Large
25. Staff	Minimal				Large

Figure A-6 (cont.): Management Capability Profile

Target Duration of Programs (Years): _____

Changes in Marketing Strategy: _____

Changes in Innovation Strategy: _____

Changes in General Management Capability: _____

Program Costs ($):

Formulating and Implementing New Strategies: _____

Transforming General Management Capability: _____

Programs	Gap	Program Priorities	% Budget for Transformation	
			First Year	Last Year
1. Marketing Strategy				
2. Innovation Strategy				
3. Development of Key Managers				
4. Development of Culture				
5. Management Info. System Changes				
6. Structural Changes				
7. Power Structure Changes				
8. Decision System Changes				
9. Development of New Analytical Models and Computer Applications				
10. Changes in Managerial Capacity (in numbers of general managers)				
11. Other				
12. Other				
	100%	100%	100%	100%

Figure A-7: Program Priorities for Strategic Posture Transformation

Programs

Timing (Years)*

	1	2	3	4	5	6	7	8	9	10
1. Marketing Strategy										
2. Strategy of Innovation through Internal Development Strategy										
3. Strategy of Innovation through Acquisitions										
4. Development of Key Managers										
5. Development of Culture										
6. Management Information System Changes										
7. Structural Changes										
8. Power Structure										
9. Systems Changes										
10. Development of New Analytical Models and Computer Applications										
11. Changes in Managerial Capacity (in numbers of general managers)										
12. Other										
13. Other										

* Draw a line opposite each program which starts at the time of initiation and stops at time of termination of the program.

Figure A-8: Plan for Strategic Transformation

What Are the Potential Problems?	What Should Be Done?	Who Should Do It?

Figure A-9: Measures to Assure Effective Implementation

Appendix B
COMPANY ANALYSIS

Each company was analyzed using the following steps:
1. The company information was read to identify whether it fulfills the criteria for analysis.
2. Information concerning companies that fulfilled the criteria was read again and some points of the instrument were answered.
3. Preliminary financial data was collected about company performance.
4. A complete read-out and analysis of the company followed, filling out all possible parts and questions of the instrument.
5. The company was screened to identify the criteria of applicability.
6. If necessary, additional financial information was collected about the company from the Moody's Industrial Manual.
7. Financial data of the performance of the industry were collected from the Dun and Bradstreet *Key Business Ratios* for the same Standard Industrial Classification (SIC) Code and for the same financial period.
8. Figure B-3 of the instrument was applied to identify the posture analysis of the company.
9. The company was classified into one of the following groups:
    a. Companies belonging to the manufacturing or wholesale/retail SIC Classification.
    b. The existence or not of gap for each of the three types of gap examined in the present study.
       1) Environmental turbulence and strategic aggressiveness.
       2) Environmental turbulence and general management capability.
       3) Environmental turbulence and strategic aggressiveness in combination with general management capability.
10. The count, mean and standard deviation was calculated for each of the groups and for the industry that the company belonged to for a period of four years.
11. Companies were classified into performing better and worse than the industry to which they belonged by comparing the findings of the mean and standard deviation with that of the industry.

Where a division of a larger firm was analyzed, only the SIC codes of that division were used; a firm known as a retailer may be listed under manufacturing if it had a manufacturing division that was studied. A firm known as a manufacturer may be listed under wholesale/retail if it has a wholesale or retail unit that was studied.

A posture analysis of the Kroehler Manufacturing Company follows, where key phrases and words correspond to each level and part of the instrument.

Company Name: Kroehler Manufacturing Company   <u>Furniture Manufacturer</u>

> Environmental turbulence vs. strategic aggressiveness: No Gap
> Environmental turbulence vs. general management capability: No Gap
> Environmental turbulence vs. strategic aggressiveness in combination with general management capability: No Gap

Source: Wheelen, T. L. and J. D. Hunger. *Strategic Management and Business Policy*. Reading, Mass.: Addison-Wesley, 1983, p. 783.

Attribute	Level	Case Abstracts
1. % of Industry Profit Spent On Marketing	D	
2. Market Structure	D	Furniture imported is triple the amount exported. p. 741
3. Aggressiveness of Leading Competitors	C-D	Sales are normally made ahead of production. p. 741
4. Pressure by Customers	D	One manufacturer's innovation or designs are rapidly adopted by competitors. p. 744
5. <u>Demand</u> Industry Capacity	C-D	
6. Stage in Industry Life Cycle	C	
7. Profitability	C-D	
8. Product Differentiation	D	Influx of foreign influence.
9. Critical Marketing Success Factors	C-D	New trends in style and patterns.

Figure B-1: Levels of Marketing Turbulence

Attribute	Level	Case Abstracts
1. % of Industry Sales Spent on R & D		
2. Frequency of New Products in Industry	D-S	Need of patent—p. 774: Imported products.
3. Product Life Cycles	C-D	Improving levels of disposable personal income and the decreasing unemployment rate. p. 743
4. Rate of Change of Technology	C-D	Change in the designs of fabrics, mainly.
5. Diversity of Competing Technology	C	The concentration is only on the production of new designs and new fabrics.
6. Stage of Industry Life Cycle	C	
7. Profitability	C-D	
8. Critical Innovation Success Factor	C-D	

The company analysis should include adequate information to analyze the levels of marketing and innovation turbulence. In the case of Kroehler Manufacturing Company, the levels of turbulence were within the changing and discontinuous levels. This did not call for registering the existence of a gap. The information gathered from Figures B-1 and B-2 was plotted into Figure B-3 under marketing turbulence and innovation turbulence.

Figure B-2: Levels of Innovation Turbulence

Appendix C
DATA SOURCES

The company information was found in the following books:

Baughman, J. P. et al. *Environmental Analysis for Management*. Homewood, Ill.: R. D. Irwin, 1974.

Brulton, W. *Business Policy*. New York: MacMillan Publications, Inc., 1984.

Christensen, R. *Business Policy: Text and Cases*. Homewood, Ill.: R. D. Irwin, 1982.

Glueck, W. F. *Business Policy and Strategic Management*. New York: McGraw Hill, 1984.

Glueck, W. F. *Business Policy*. New York: McGraw-Hill, Inc., 1976.

Hodgetts, R. M. *Administrative Policy: Text and Cases in Strategic Management*. New York: Wiley, 1980.

Hofer, C. W., E. A. Murray, Jr., P. Charan and R. Pitts. *Strategic Management: A Casebook in Policy and Planning*. Santa Clara, Ca.: West Publishing Co., 1984.

McNichols, T. J. *Policy Making and Executive Action*. New York: McGraw-Hill, 1983.

Naumes, W. and F. T. Paine. *Cases for Organizational Strategy and Policy*. U.S.A.: W. B. Saunders Company, 1978.

Steiner, G. A. *Management Policy and Strategy*. New York: MacMillan Publishing Co., Inc., 1982.

Thompson, A. A., Jr. *Strategy and Policy, Concepts and Cases*. Dallas, Texas: Business Publications Inc., 1978.

Thompson, A. A., Jr. and A. J. Strickland, III. *Strategic Management: Concepts and Cases*. Dallas, Texas: Business Publications Inc., 1984.

Uyterhoven, H. E. *Strategy and Organization. Text and Cases in General Management*. Homewood, Ill.: R. D. Irwin, 1977.

Wheelen, T. L and J. D. Hunger. *Strategic Management and Business Policy*. Reading, Mass.: Addison-Wesley Publishing Co., Inc., 1983.

Appendix D
DATA ANALYSIS OF
THE THREE TYPES OF GAP

Gap 1: Environmental turbulence and strategic aggressiveness.
Gap 2: Environmental turbulence and general management capability.
Gap 3: Environmental turbulence and strategic aggressiveness in combination with general management capability.

Ratio 1: Sales to net worth for company
Ratio 2: Sales to net worth for industry
Ratio 3: Net profit to sales for company
Ratio 4: Net profit to sales for industry

As mentioned previously, in certain cases where a company was a subsidiary of a corporation, only the data for the subsidiary or the division was collected and analyzed.

Group 1
Manufacturing Companies With Gap 1: Environment & Strategy

Company	Ratio1	Ratio2	R2-R1	Ratio3	Ratio4	R4-R3
Alabama Power	0.860	0.775	-0.085	8.688	4.533	-4.155
American Auto. Typewriter	0.479	3.487	3.008	1.290	2.442	1.152
ARMCO	1.931	2.785	0.854	3.912	4.667	0.755
Bishopric Inc.	3.952	3.040	-0.912	8.211	3.915	-4.296
Edison	0.851	3.650	2.799	0.996	3.640	2.644
Gerber Food	2.587	3.970	1.383	5.500	2.960	-2.540
L. L. Bean	4.056	2.482	-1.574	5.881	2.770	-3.111
L.T.V.	1.546	2.840	1.294	1.710	4.240	2.530
Marion Lab	1.579	3.475	1.896	1.090	5.022	3.932
Mead	2.765	2.820	0.055	3.790	3.500	-0.290
Norton	2.051	4.027	1.976	4.283	2.335	-1.948
Richmond Brick	3.932	2.627	-1.305	4.012	3.402	-0.610
The Washington Post	1.967	2.012	0.045	5.251	3.565	-1.686
Tracor	4.634	3.360	-1.272	4.182	5.942	1.760
United Technologies	3.856	2.275	-1.581	3.500	3.403	-0.097
Webber	5.375	4.987	-0.388	6.325	3.185	-3.140
COUNT	16	16	16	16	16	16
MEAN	2.651	3.038	0.387	4.289	3.720	-0.569
STANDARD DEV.	1.436	0.932	1.492	2.259	0.939	2.468

Group 2
Manufacturing Companies Without Gap 1: Environment & Strategy

Company	Ratio1	Ratio2	R2-R1	Ratio3	Ratio4	R4-R3
ADCOMP	4.344	2.530	-1.814	5.033	3.840	-1.193
Advanced Computers	1.359	2.865	1.506	5.033	3.827	-1.206
AMCO	1.856	1.925	0.069	8.336	6.375	-1.961
Apple	3.176	1.756	-1.420	1.072	4.367	3.295
Ashland Oil	5.505	5.502	-0.003	4.694	3.047	-1.647
Avon	1.591	2.055	0.464	11.392	6.215	-5.177
Calma	3.451	3.100	-0.351	6.310	5.840	-0.470
Clark Oil	7.156	6.100	-1.056	3.257	3.251	-0.006
Dictaphone	3.289	1.937	-1.352	3.826	3.266	-0.560
Dr. Pepper	2.853	2.735	-0.118	7.761	5.637	-2.124
Harlequin	2.602	2.025	-0.577	1.133	4.762	3.629
Hewlett-Packard	1.278	1.537	0.259	8.652	5.547	-3.105
Independent Publ. Co.	1.375	2.012	0.637	2.495	4.315	1.820
Johnson Products	1.404	2.382	0.978	0.900	2.275	1.375
Kramer	5.379	3.087	-2.292	1.379	3.160	1.781
Kroehler	3.100	3.280	0.180	2.505	2.535	0.030
Lincoln Electric	2.341	3.125	0.784	8.076	5.102	-2.974
Mary Kay	1.969	1.800	-0.169	12.529	6.155	-6.374
Medford	5.523	4.777	-0.746	0.193	2.675	2.482
Modern Publishing Co.	1.793	2.091	0.298	5.801	4.447	-1.354
Polaroid	1.384	1.400	0.016	7.100	2.320	-4.780
Royal Crown	3.296	2.700	-0.596	5.257	5.637	0.380
Seven Up	18.466	3.472	-14.994	9.433	5.837	-3.596
Standard Oil	4.228	2.453	-1.775	2.250	3.852	1.602
Techtronics	1.963	2.972	1.009	1.879	3.927	2.048
Texas Instruments	2.088	3.212	1.124	5.408	5.547	0.139
Virginia Chemicals	2.834	2.905	0.071	2.763	2.572	-0.191
COUNT	27	27	27	27	27	27
MEAN	3.541	2.805	-0.736	4.980	4.309	-0.672
STANDARD DEV.	3.291	1.107	2.051	3.269	1.309	2.519

Group 3
Wholesale/Retail Companies With Gap 1: Environment & Strategy

Company	Ratio 1	Ratio 2	R2-R1	Ratio 3	Ratio 4	R4-R3
American Motors	7.580	3.175	-4.405	3.000	3.520	0.520
Anheuser-Bush	3.265	2.600	-0.665	3.900	1.960	-1.940
Bartl's	1.762	8.290	6.528	2.195	2.407	0.212
Chrysler	5.051	3.050	-2.001	1.513	2.680	1.167
Fleetwood	7.921	3.977	-3.944	4.233	2.400	-1.833
Hersey	2.711	12.747	10.036	0.817	0.737	-0.080
Joseph Schlitz	2.059	2.550	0.491	0.203	2.243	2.040
Taylor Wine	1.054	8.015	6.961	2.145	1.723	-0.422
COUNT	8	8	8	8	8	8
MEAN	3.925	5.551	1.625	2.251	2.209	-0.042
STANDARD DEV.	2.473	3.490	5.127	1.324	0.749	1.281

Group 4
Wholesale/Retail Companies Without Gap 1: Environment & Strategy

Company	Ratio 1	Ratio 2	R2-R1	Ratio 3	Ratio 4	R4-R3
Albertsons Inc.	11.970	3.355	-8.615	1.158	2.240	1.082
Coastal Chemical	1.175	6.017	4.842	3.451	3.120	-0.331
Cottage Gardens	52.104	12.125	-39.980	4.687	4.796	0.109
Kellwood	6.768	2.585	-4.183	1.675	2.600	0.925
Mint Flavors	8.303	7.897	-0.406	2.330	2.920	0.590
The Southland Corp.	7.357	10.775	3.418	1.862	1.475	-0.387
VW	2.073	4.382	2.309	2.699	3.097	0.398
Winnebago	2.494	3.350	0.856	0.872	3.097	2.225
COUNT	8	8	8	8	8	8
MEAN	11.531	6.311	-5.220	2.342	2.918	0.576
STANDARD DEV.	15.713	3.381	13.754	1.178	0.886	0.798

Group 5
Manufacturing Companies With Gap 2: Environment & Capability

Company	Ratio1	Ratio2	R2-R1	Ratio3	Ratio4	R4-R3
Alabama Power	0.860	0.775	-0.085	8.688	4.533	-4.155
American Auto. Typewriter	0.479	3.487	3.008	1.290	2.442	1.152
ARMCO	1.931	2.785	0.854	3.912	4.667	0.755
Bishopric Inc.	3.952	3.040	-0.912	8.211	3.915	-4.296
Edison	0.851	3.650	2.799	0.996	3.640	2.644
Gerber Food	2.587	3.970	1.383	5.500	2.960	-2.540
L. L. Bean	4.056	2.482	-1.574	5.881	2.770	-3.111
Mead	2.765	2.820	0.055	3.790	3.500	-0.290
Norton	2.051	4.027	1.976	4.283	2.335	-1.948
Richmond Brick	3.932	2.627	-1.305	4.012	3.402	-0.610
The Washington Post	1.967	2.012	0.045	5.251	3.565	-1.686
Tracor	4.634	3.360	-1.274	4.182	5.942	1.760
United Technologies	3.856	2.275	-1.581	3.500	3.403	-0.097
Webber	5.375	4.987	-0.388	6.325	3.185	-3.140
COUNT	14	14	14	14	14	14
MEAN	2.807	3.021	0.214	4.702	3.590	-1.112
STANDARD DEV.	1.471	0.988	1.514	2.111	0.922	2.130

Group 6
Manufacturing Companies Without Gap 2: Environment & Capability

Company	Ratio1	Ratio2	R2-R1	Ratio3	Ratio4	R4-R3
ADCOMP	4.344	2.530	-1.814	5.033	3.840	-1.193
Advanced Computers	1.359	2.865	1.506	5.033	3.827	-1.206
AMCO	1.856	1.925	0.069	8.336	6.375	-1.961
Apple	3.176	1.756	-1.420	1.072	4.367	3.295
Ashland Oil	5.505	5.502	-0.003	4.694	3.047	-1.647
Avon	1.591	2.055	0.464	11.392	6.215	-5.177
Calma	3.451	3.100	-0.351	6.310	5.840	-0.470
Clark Oil	7.156	6.100	-1.056	3.257	3.251	-0.006
Dictaphone	3.289	1.927	-1.352	3.826	3.266	-0.560
Dr. Pepper	2.853	2.735	-0.118	7.761	5.637	-2.124
Harlequin	2.602	2.025	-0.577	1.133	4.762	3.629
Hewlett-Packard	1.278	1.537	0.259	8.652	5.547	-3.105
Independent Publ. Co.	1.375	2.012	0.637	2.495	4.315	1.820
Johnson Products	1.404	2.382	0.978	0.900	2.275	1.375
Kramer	5.379	3.087	-2.292	1.379	3.160	1.781
Kroehler	3.100	3.280	0.180	2.505	2.535	0.030
Lincoln Electric	2.341	3.125	0.784	8.076	5.102	-2.974
L.T.V.	1.546	2.840	1.294	1.710	4.240	2.530
Marion Lab	1.579	3.475	1.896	1.090	5.022	3.932
Mary Kay	1.969	1.800	-0.169	12.529	6.155	-6.374
Medford	5.523	4.777	-0.746	0.193	2.675	2.482
Modern Publishing Co.	1.793	2.091	0.298	5.801	4.447	-1.354
Polaroid	1.384	1.400	0.016	7.100	2.320	-4.780
Royal Crown	3.296	2.700	-0.596	5.257	5.637	0.380
Seven Up	18.466	3.472	-14.990	9.433	5.837	-3.596
Standard Oil	4.228	2.453	-1.775	2.250	3.852	1.602
Techtronics	1.963	2.972	1.009	1.879	3.927	2.048
Texas Instruments	2.088	3.212	1.124	5.408	5.547	0.139
Virginia Chemicals	2.834	2.905	0.071	2.763	2.572	-0.191
COUNT	29	29	29	29	29	29
MEAN	3.404	2.829	-0.575	4.733	4.331	-0.403
STANDARD DEV.	3.215	1.075	2.910	3.283	1.270	2.631

Group 7
Wholesale/Retail Companies With Gap 2: Environment & Capability

Company	Ratio1	Ratio2	R2-R1	Ratio3	Ratio4	R4-R3
American Motors	7.580	3.175	-4.405	3.000	3.520	-0.520
Anheuser-Bush	3.265	2.600	-0.665	3.900	1.960	-1.940
Bartl's	1.762	8.290	6.528	2.195	2.407	0.212
Chrysler	5.051	3.050	-2.001	1.513	2.680	1.167
Fleetwood	7.921	3.977	-3.944	4.233	2.400	-1.833
Hersey	2.711	12.747	10.036	0.817	0.737	-0.080
Joseph Schlitz	2.059	2.550	0.491	0.203	2.243	2.040
Mint Flavors	8.303	7.897	-0.406	2.330	2.920	0.590
Taylor Wine	1.054	8.015	6.961	2.145	1.723	-0.422
COUNT	9	9	9	9	9	9
MEAN	4.412	5.811	1.399	2.260	2.288	0.028
STANDARD DEV.	2.707	3.372	4.876	1.248	0.740	1.224

Group 8
Wholesale/Retail Companies Without Gap 2: Environment & Capability

Company	Ratio1	Ratio2	R2-R1	Ratio3	Ratio4	R4-R3
Albertsons Inc.	11.970	3.355	-8.615	1.158	2.240	1.082
Coastal Chemical	1.175	6.017	4.842	3.451	3.120	-0.331
Cottage Gardens	52.104	12.125	-39.980	4.687	4.796	0.109
Kellwood	6.768	2.585	-4.183	1.675	2.600	0.925
The Southland Corp.	7.357	10.775	3.418	1.862	1.475	-0.387
VW	2.073	4.382	2.309	2.699	3.097	0.398
Winnebago	2.494	3.350	0.856	0.872	3.097	2.225
COUNT	7	7	7	7	7	7
MEAN	11.992	6.084	-5.907	2.343	2.918	0.574
STANDARD DEV.	16.748	3.557	14.575	1.259	0.947	0.853

Group 9
Manufacturing Companies With Gap 3:
Environment & Strategy With Capability

Company	Ratio1	Ratio2	R2-R1	Ratio3	Ratio4	R4-R3
Advanced Computers	1.359	2.865	1.506	5.033	3.827	-1.206
Alabama Power	0.860	0.775	-0.085	8.688	4.533	-4.155
American Auto. Typewriter	0.479	3.487	3.008	1.290	2.442	1.152
ARMCO	1.931	2.785	0.854	3.912	4.667	0.755
Bishopric Inc.	3.952	3.040	-0.912	8.211	3.915	-4.296
Edison	0.851	3.650	2.799	0.996	3.640	2.644
Gerber Food	2.587	3.976	1.383	5.500	2.960	-2.540
Johnson Products	1.404	2.382	0.978	0.900	2.275	1.375
L. L. Bean	4.056	2.482	-1.574	5.881	2.770	-3.111
L.T.V.	1.546	2.840	1.294	1.710	4.240	2.530
Marion Lab	1.579	3.475	1.896	1.090	5.022	3.932
Mead	2.765	2.820	0.055	3.790	3.500	-0.290
Medord	5.523	4.777	-0.746	0.193	2.675	2.482
Norton	2.051	4.027	1.976	4.283	2.335	-1.948
Richmond Brick	3.932	2.627	-1.305	4.012	3.402	-0.610
Standard Oil	4.228	2.453	-1.775	2.250	3.852	1.602
Techtronics	1.963	2.972	1.009	1.879	3.927	2.048
The Washington Post	1.967	2.012	0.045	5.251	3.565	-1.686
Tracor	4.634	3.360	-1.274	4.182	5.942	1.760
United Technologies	3.856	2.275	-1.581	3.500	3.403	-0.097
Webber	5.375	4.987	-0.388	6.325	3.185	-3.140
COUNT	21	21	21	21	21	21
MEAN	2.709	3.051	0.341	3.756	3.623	-0.133
STANDARD DEV.	1.502	0.919	1.439	2.334	0.904	2.376

Group 10
Manufacturing Companies Without Gap 3:
Environment & Strategy With Capability

Company	Ratio1	Ratio2	R2-R1	Ratio3	Ratio4	R4-R3
ADCOMP	4.344	2.530	-1.814	5.033	3.840	-1.193
AMCO	1.856	1.925	0.069	8.336	6.375	-1.961
Apple	3.176	1.756	-1.420	1.072	4.367	3.295
Ashland Oil	5.505	5.502	-0.003	4.694	3.047	-1.647
Avon	1.591	2.055	0.464	11.392	6.215	-5.177
Calma	3.451	3.100	-0.351	6.310	5.840	-0.470
Clark Oil	7.156	6.100	-1.056	3.257	3.251	-0.006
Dictaphone	3.289	1.937	-1.352	3.826	3.266	-0.560
Dr. Pepper	2.853	2.735	-0.118	7.761	5.637	-2.124
Harlequin	2.602	2.025	-0.577	1.133	4.762	3.629
Hewlett-Packard	1.278	1.537	0.259	8.652	5.547	-3.105
Independent Publ. Co.	1.375	2.012	0.637	2.495	4.315	1.820
Kramer	5.379	3.087	-2.292	1.370	3.160	1.781
Kroehler	3.100	3.280	0.180	2.505	2.535	0.030
Lincoln Electric	2.341	3.125	0.784	8.076	5.102	-2.974
Mary Kay	1.969	1.800	-0.169	12.529	6.155	-6.374
Modern Publishing Co.	1.793	2.091	0.298	5.801	4.447	-1.354
Polaroid	1.384	1.400	0.016	7.100	2.320	-4.780
Royal Crown	3.296	2.700	-0.596	5.257	5.637	0.380
Seven Up	18.466	3.472	-14.990	9.433	5.837	-3.596
Texas Instruments	2.088	3.212	1.124	5.408	5.547	0.139
Virginia Chemicals	2.834	2.905	0.071	2.763	2.572	-0.191
COUNT	22	22	22	22	22	22
MEAN	3.688	2.740	-0.947	5.646	4.535	-1.111
STANDARD DEV.	3.540	1.144	3.178	3.177	1.310	2.524

Group 11
Wholesale/Retail Companies With Gap 3:
Environment & Strategy With Capability

Company	Ratio1	Ratio2	R2-R1	Ratio3	Ratio4	R4-R3
American Motors	7.580	3.175	-4.405	3.000	3.520	0.520
Anheuser–Busch	3.265	2.600	-0.665	3.900	1.960	-1.940
Bartl's	1.762	8.290	6.528	2.195	2.407	0.212
Chrysler	5.051	3.050	-2.001	1.513	2.680	1.167
Fleetwood	7.921	3.977	-3.944	4.233	2.400	-1.833
Hersey	2.711	12.747	10.036	0.817	0.737	-0.080
Joseph Schlitz	2.059	2.550	0.491	0.203	2.243	2.040
Mint Flavors	8.303	7.891	-0.406	2.330	2.920	0.590
Taylor Wine	1.054	8.015	6.961	2.145	1.723	-0.422
COUNT	9	9	9	9	9	9
MEAN	4.412	5.811	1.399	2.260	2.288	0.028
STANDARD DEV.	2.707	3.372	4.876	1.248	0.740	1.224

Group 12
Wholesale/Retail Companies Without Gap 3:
Environment & Strategy With Capability

Company	Ratio1	Ratio2	R2-R1	Ratio3	Ratio4	R4-R3
Albertsons Inc.	11.970	3.355	-8.615	1.158	2.240	1.082
Coastal Chemical	1.175	6.017	4.842	3.451	3.120	-0.331
Cottage Gardens	52.104	12.125	-39.980	4.687	4.796	0.109
Kellwood	6.768	2.585	-4.183	1.675	2.600	0.925
The Southland Corp.	7.357	10.775	3.418	1.862	1.475	-0.387
VW	2.073	4.382	2.309	2.699	3.097	0.398
Winnebago	2.494	3.350	0.856	0.872	3.097	2.225
COUNT	7	7	7	7	7	7
MEAN	11.992	6.084	-5.907	2.343	2.918	0.574
STANDARD DEV.	16.748	3.557	14.575	1.259	0.947	0.853

Group 13
All Companies With Gap 1: Environment & Strategy

Company	Ratio1	Ratio2	R2-R1	Ratio3	Ratio4	R4-R3
Alabama Power	0.860	0.775	–0.085	8.688	4.533	–4.155
American Auto. Typewriter	0.479	3.487	3.008	1.290	2.442	1.152
American Motors	7.580	3.175	–4.405	3.000	3.520	0.520
Anheuser–Bush	3.265	2.600	–0.665	3.900	1.960	–1.940
ARMCO	1.931	2.785	0.854	3.912	4.667	0.755
Bartl's	1.762	8.290	6.528	2.195	2.407	0.212
Bishopric Inc.	3.952	3.040	–0.912	8.211	3.915	–4.296
Chrysler	5.051	3.050	–2.001	1.513	2.680	1.167
Edison	0.851	3.650	2.799	0.996	3.640	2.644
Fleetwood	7.921	3.977	–3.944	4.233	2.400	–1.833
Gerber Food	2.587	3.970	1.383	5.500	2.960	–2.540
Hersey	2.711	12.747	10.036	0.817	0.737	–0.080
Joseph Schlitz	2.059	2.550	0.491	0.203	2.243	2.040
L. L. Bean	4.056	2.482	–1.574	5.881	2.770	–3.111
L.T.V.	1.546	2.840	1.294	1.710	4.240	2.530
Marion Lab	1.579	3.475	1.896	1.090	5.022	3.932
Mead	2.765	2.820	0.055	3.790	3.500	–0.290
Norton	2.051	4.027	1.976	4.283	2.335	–1.948
Richmond Brick	3.932	2.627	–1.305	4.012	3.402	–0.610
Taylor Wine	1.054	8.015	6.961	2.145	1.723	–0.422
The Washington Post	1.967	2.012	0.045	5.251	3.565	–1.686
Tracor	4.634	3.360	–1.274	4.182	5.942	1.760
United Technologies	3.856	2.275	–1.581	3.500	3.403	–0.097
Webber	5.375	4.987	–0.388	6.325	3.185	–3.140
COUNT	24	24	24	24	24	24
MEAN	3.076	3.876	0.800	3.609	3.216	–0.393
STANDARD DEV.	1.943	2.458	3.254	2.215	1.132	2.161

Group 14
All Companies Without Gap 1: Environment & Strategy

Company	Ratio1	Ratio2	R2-R1	Ratio3	Ratio4	R4-R3
ADCOMP	4.344	2.530	-1.814	5.033	3.840	-1.193
Advanced Computers	1.359	2.865	1.506	5.033	3.827	-1.206
Albertsons Inc.	11.970	3.355	-8.615	1.158	2.240	1.082
AMCO	1.856	1.925	0.069	8.336	6.475	-1.961
Apple	3.176	1.756	-1.420	1.072	4.367	3.295
Ashland Oil	5.505	5.502	-0.003	4.694	3.047	-1.647
Avon	1.591	2.055	0.464	11.392	6.215	-5.177
Calma	3.451	3.100	-0.351	6.310	5.840	-0.470
Clark Oil	7.156	6.100	-1.056	3.257	3.251	-0.006
Coastal Chemical	1.175	6.017	4.842	3.451	3.120	-0.331
Cottage Gardens	52.104	12.125	-39.980	4.687	4.796	0.109
Dictaphone	3.289	1.937	-1.352	3.826	3.266	-0.560
Dr. Pepper	2.853	2.735	-0.118	7.761	5.637	-2.124
Harlequin	2.602	2.025	-0.577	1.133	4.762	3.629
Hewlett-Packard	1.278	1.537	0.259	8.652	5.547	-3.105
Independent Publ. Co.	1.375	2.012	0.637	2.495	4.315	1.820
Johnson Products	1.404	2.382	0.978	0.900	2.275	1.375
Kellwood	6.768	2.585	-4.183	1.675	2.600	0.925
Kramer	5.379	3.087	-2.292	1.379	3.160	1.781
Kroehler	3.100	3.280	0.180	2.505	2.535	0.030
Lincoln Electric	2.341	3.125	0.784	8.076	5.102	-2.974
Mary Kay	1.969	1.800	-0.169	12.529	6.155	-6.374
Medford	5.523	4.777	-0.746	0.193	2.675	2.482
Mint Flavors	8.303	7.897	-0.406	2.330	2.920	0.590
Modern Publishing Co.	1.793	2.091	0.298	5.801	4.447	-1.354
Polaroid	1.384	1.400	0.016	7.100	2.320	-4.780
Royal Crown	3.296	2.700	-0.596	5.257	5.637	0.380
Seven Up	18.466	3.472	-14.990	9.433	5.837	-3.596
Standard Oil	4.228	2.453	-1.775	2.250	3.852	1.602
Techtronics	1.963	2.972	1.009	1.879	3.927	2.048
Texas Instruments	2.088	3.212	1.124	5.408	5.547	0.139
The Southland Corp.	7.357	10.775	3.418	1.862	1.475	-0.387
Virginia Chemicals	2.834	2.905	0.071	2.763	2.572	-0.191
VW	2.073	4.382	2.309	2.699	3.097	0.398
Winnebago	2.494	3.350	0.856	0.872	3.097	2.225
COUNT	35	35	35	35	35	35
MEAN	5.367	3.606	-1.761	4.377	3.991	-0.386
STANDARD DEV.	8.720	2.393	7.315	3.128	1.357	2.306

Group 15
All Companies With Gap 2: Environment & Capability

Company	Ratio1	Ratio2	R2-R1	Ratio3	Ratio4	R4-R3
Alabama Power	0.860	0.775	-0.085	8.688	4.533	-4.155
American Auto. Typewriter	0.479	3.487	3.008	1.290	2.442	1.152
American Motors	7.580	3.175	-4.405	3.000	3.520	0.520
Anheuser-Bush	3.265	2.600	-0.665	3.900	1.960	-1.940
ARMCO	1.931	2.785	0.854	3.912	4.667	0.755
Bartl's	1.762	8.290	6.528	2.195	2.407	0.212
Bishopric Inc.	3.952	3.040	-0.912	8.211	3.915	-4.296
Chrysler	5.051	3.050	-2.001	1.513	2.680	1.167
Edison	0.851	3.650	2.799	0.996	3.640	2.644
Fleetwood	7.921	3.977	-3.944	4.233	2.400	-1.833
Gerber Food	2.587	3.970	1.383	5.500	2.960	-2.540
Hersey	2.711	12.747	10.036	0.817	0.737	-0.080
Joseph Schlitz	2.059	2.550	0.491	0.203	2.243	2.040
L. L. Bean	4.056	2.482	-1.574	5.881	2.770	-3.111
Mead	2.765	2.820	0.055	3.790	3.500	-0.290
Mint Flavors	8.303	7.897	-0.406	2.330	2.920	0.590
Norton	2.051	4.027	1.976	4.283	2.335	-1.948
Richmond Brick	3.932	2.627	-1.305	4.012	3.402	-0.610
Taylor Wine	1.054	8.015	6.961	2.145	1.723	-0.422
The Washington Post	1.967	2.012	0.045	5.251	3.565	-1.686
Tracor	4.634	3.360	-1.274	4.182	5.942	1.760
United Technologies	3.856	2.275	-1.581	3.500	3.403	-0.097
Webber	5.375	4.987	-0.388	6.325	3.185	-3.140
COUNT	23	23	23	23	23	23
MEAN	3.435	4.113	0.678	3.746	3.080	-0.666
STANDARD DEV.	2.190	2.626	3.322	2.177	1.066	1.912

Group 16
All Companies Without Gap 2: Environment & Capability

Company	Ratio1	Ratio2	R2-R1	Ratio3	Ratio4	R4-R3
ADCOMP	4.344	2.530	-1.814	5.033	3.840	-1.193
Advanced Computers	1.359	2.865	1.506	5.033	3.827	-1.206
Albertsons Inc.	11.970	3.355	-8.615	1.158	2.240	1.082
AMCO	1.856	1.925	0.069	8.336	6.375	-1.961
Apple	3.176	1.756	-1.420	1.072	4.367	3.295
Ashland Oil	5.505	5.502	-0.003	4.694	3.047	-1.647
Avon	1.591	2.055	0.464	11.392	6.215	-5.177
Calma	3.451	3.100	-0.351	6.310	5.840	-0.470
Clark Oil	7.156	6.100	-1.056	3.257	3.251	-0.006
Coastal Chemical	1.175	6.017	4.842	3.451	3.120	-0.331
Cottage Gardens	52.104	12.125	-39.980	4.687	4.796	0.109
Dictaphone	3.289	1.937	-1.352	3.826	3.266	-0.560
Dr. Pepper	2.853	2.735	-0.118	7.761	5.637	-2.124
Harlequin	2.602	2.025	-0.577	1.133	4.762	3.629
Hewlett-Packard	1.278	1.537	0.259	8.652	5.547	-3.105
Independent Publ. Co.	1.375	2.012	0.637	2.495	4.315	1.820
Johnson Products	1.404	2.382	0.978	0.900	2.275	1.375
Kellwood	6.768	2.585	-4.183	1.675	2.600	0.925
Kramer	5.379	3.087	-2.292	1.379	3.160	1.781
Kroehler	3.100	3.280	0.180	2.505	2.535	0.030
Lincoln Electric	2.341	3.125	0.784	8.076	5.102	-2.974
L.T.V.	1.546	2.840	1.294	1.710	4.240	2.530
Marion Lab	1.579	3.475	1.896	1.090	5.022	3.932
Mary Kay	1.969	1.800	-0.169	12.529	6.155	-6.374
Medford	5.523	4.777	-0.746	0.193	2.675	2.482
Modern Publishing Co.	1.793	2.091	0.298	5.801	4.447	-1.354
Polaroid	1.384	1.400	0.016	7.100	2.320	-4.780
Royal Crown	3.296	2.700	-0.596	5.257	5.637	0.380
Seven Up	18.466	3.472	-14.990	9.433	5.837	-3.596
Standard Oil	4.228	2.453	-1.775	2.250	3.852	1.602
Techtronics	1.963	2.972	1.009	1.879	3.927	2.048
Texas Instruments	2.088	3.212	1.124	5.408	5.547	0.139
The Southland Corp.	7.357	10.775	3.418	1.862	1.475	-0.387
Virginia Chemicals	2.834	2.905	0.071	2.763	2.572	-0.191
VW	2.073	4.382	2.309	2.699	3.097	0.398
Winnebago	2.494	3.350	0.856	0.872	3.097	2.225
COUNT	36	36	36	36	36	36
MEAN	5.074	3.462	-1.612	4.269	4.056	-0.213
STANDARD DEV.	8.626	2.247	7.251	3.144	1.337	2.422

Group 17
All Companies With Gap 3: Environment & Strategy With Capability

Company	Ratio1	Ratio2	R2-R1	Ratio3	Ratio4	R4-R3
Advanced Computers	1.359	2.865	1.506	5.033	3.827	-1.206
Alabama Power	0.860	0.775	-0.085	8.688	4.533	-4.155
American Auto. Typewriter	0.479	3.487	3.008	1.290	2.442	1.152
American Motors	7.580	3.175	-4.405	3.000	3.520	0.520
Anheuser-Bush	3.265	2.600	-0.665	3.900	1.960	-1.940
ARMCO	1.931	2.785	0.854	3.912	4.667	0.755
Bartl's	1.762	8.290	6.528	2.195	2.407	0.212
Bishopric Inc.	3.952	3.040	-0.912	8.211	3.915	-4.296
Chrysler	5.051	3.050	-2.001	1.513	2.680	1.167
Edison	0.851	3.650	2.799	0.996	3.640	2.644
Fleetwood	7.921	3.977	-3.944	4.233	2.400	-1.833
Gerber Food	2.587	3.970	1.383	5.500	2.960	-2.540
Hersey	2.711	12.747	10.036	0.817	0.737	-0.080
Johnson Products	1.404	2.382	0.978	0.900	2.275	1.375
Joseph Schlitz	2.059	2.550	0.491	0.203	2.243	2.040
L. L. Bean	4.056	2.482	-1.574	5.881	2.770	-3.111
L.T.V.	1.546	2.840	1.294	1.710	4.240	2.530
Marion Lab	1.579	3.475	1.896	1.090	5.022	3.932
Mead	2.765	2.820	0.055	3.790	3.500	-0.290
Medford	5.523	4.777	-0.746	0.193	2.675	2.482
Mint Flavors	8.303	7.897	-0.406	2.330	2.920	0.590
Norton	2.051	4.027	1.976	4.282	2.335	-1.948
Richmond Brick	3.932	2.627	-1.305	4.012	3.402	-0.610
Standard Oil	4.228	2.453	-1.775	2.250	3.852	1.602
Taylor Wine	1.054	8.015	6.961	2.145	1.723	-0.422
Techtronics	1.963	2.972	1.009	1.879	3.927	2.048
The Washington Post	1.967	2.012	0.045	5.251	3.565	-1.686
Tracor	4.634	3.360	-1.274	4.182	5.942	1.760
United Technologies	3.856	2.275	-1.581	3.500	3.403	-0.097
Webber	5.375	4.987	-0.388	6.325	3.185	-3.140
COUNT	30	30	30	30	30	30
MEAN	3.220	3.879	0.659	3.307	3.222	-0.085
STANDARD DEV.	2.094	2.367	2.969	2.180	1.054	2.099

Group 18
All Companies Without Gap 3: Environment & Strategy With Capability

Company	Ratio1	Ratio2	R2-R1	Ratio3	Ratio4	R4-R3
ADCOMP	4.344	2.530	-1.814	5.033	3.840	-1.193
Albertsons Inc.	11.970	3.355	-8.615	1.158	2.240	1.082
AMCO	1.856	1.925	0.069	8.336	6.375	-1.961
Apple	3.176	1.756	-1.420	1.072	4.367	3.295
Ashland Oil	5.505	5.502	-0.003	4.694	3.047	-1.647
Avon	1.591	2.055	0.464	-11.392	6.215	-5.177
Calma	3.451	3.100	-0.351	6.310	5.840	-0.470
Clark Oil	7.156	6.100	-1.056	3.257	3.251	-0.006
Coastal Chemical	1.175	6.017	4.842	3.451	3.120	-0.331
Cottage Gardens	52.104	12.125	-39.980	4.687	4.796	0.109
Dictaphone	3.289	1.937	-1.352	3.826	3.266	-0.560
Dr. Pepper	2.853	2.735	-0.118	7.761	5.637	-2.124
Harlequin	2.602	2.025	-0.577	1.133	4.762	3.629
Hewlett-Packard	1.278	1.537	0.259	8.652	5.547	-3.105
Independent Publ. Co.	1.375	2.012	0.637	2.495	4.315	1.820
Kellwood	6.768	2.585	-4.183	1.675	2.600	0.925
Kramer	5.379	3.087	-2.292	1.379	3.160	1.781
Kroehler	3.100	3.280	0.180	2.505	2.535	0.030
Lincoln Electric	2.341	3.125	0.784	8.076	5.102	-2.974
Mary Kay	1.969	1.800	-0.169	12.529	6.155	-6.374
Modern Publishing Co.	1.793	2.091	0.298	5.801	4.447	-1.354
Polaroid	1.384	1.400	0.016	7.100	2.320	-4.780
Royal Crown	3.296	2.700	-0.596	5.257	5.637	0.380
Seven Up	18.466	3.472	-14.990	9.433	5.837	-3.596
Texas Instruments	2.088	3.212	1.124	5.408	5.547	0.139
The Southland Corp.	7.357	10.775	3.418	1.862	1.475	-0.387
Virginia Chemicals	2.834	2.905	0.071	2.763	2.572	-0.191
VW	2.073	4.382	2.309	2.699	3.097	0.398
Winnebago	2.494	3.350	0.856	0.872	3.097	2.225
COUNT	29	29	29	29	29	29
MEAN	5.692	3.547	-2.145	4.849	4.145	-0.704
STANDARD DEV.	9.478	2.469	7.965	3.168	1.413	2.351

Gap 1:   Environmental turbulence and strategic aggressiveness
Gap 2:   Environmental turbulence and general management capability
Gap 3:   Environmental turbulence and strategic aggressiveness in
             combination with general management capability

Ratio 1:   Sales to net worth for company   (four-year average)
Ratio 2:   Sales to net worth for industry   (four-year average)
Ratio 3:   Net profit to sales for company   (four-year average)
Ratio 4:   Net profit to sales for industry   (four-year average)

R2-R1:   Ratio 2 – Ratio 1
R4-R3:   Ratio 4 – Ratio 3

1.	Group	1	– Manufacturing Companies With Gap 1
2.	Group	2	– Manufacturing Companies Without Gap 1
3.	Group	3	– Wholesale/Retail Companies With Gap 1
4.	Group	4	– Wholesale/Retail Companies Without Gap 1
5.	Group	13	– All Companies With Gap 1
6.	Group	14	– All Companies Without Gap 1
7.	Group	5	– Manufacturing Companies With Gap 2
8.	Group	6	– Manufacturing Companies Without Gap 2
9.	Group	7	– Wholesale/Retail Companies With Gap 2
10.	Group	8	– Wholesale/Retail Companies Without Gap 2
11.	Group	15	– All Companies With Gap 2
12.	Group	16	– All Companies Without Gap 2
13.	Group	9	– Manufacturing Companies With Gap 3
14.	Group	10	– Manufacturing Companies Without Gap 3
15.	Group	11	– Wholesale/Retail Companies With Gap 3
16.	Group	12	– Wholesale/Retail Companies Without Gap 3
17.	Group	17	– All Companies With Gap 3
18.	Group	18	– All Companies Without Gap 3

Appendix E
MANN-WHITNEY U TESTS

Mann-Whitney U Test for Calculations of Difference in Net Profit to Sales

Comparison			m	n	T	W	$E(W)$	$SD(W)$	Random Variable	Significance
Group 1	vs.	Group 2	16	27	349	219	216.0	39.8	0.075	N/S
Group 1	vs.	Group 3	8	16	111	53	64.0	16.3	-0.674	N/S
Group 2	vs.	Group 4	8	27	181	71	108.0	25.5	-1.453	80.0%
Group 3	vs.	Group 4	8	8	59	41	32.0	9.5	0.945	60.0%
Group 13	vs.	Group 14	24	35	707	433	420.0	64.8	0.201	N/S
Group 5	vs.	Group 6	14	29	267	244	203.0	38.6	1.063	70.0%
Group 5	vs.	Group 7	9	14	130	41	63.0	15.9	-1.386	80.0%
Group 6	vs.	Group 8	7	29	154	77	101.5	25.0	-0.979	60.0%
Group 7	vs.	Group 8	7	9	66	25	31.5	9.4	-0.688	50.0%
Group 15	vs.	Group 16	23	36	633	471	414.0	64.3	0.886	60.0%
Group 9	vs.	Group 10	21	22	507	186	231.0	41.2	-1.093	70.0%
Group 9	vs.	Group 11	9	21	139	95	94.5	22.1	0.023	N/S
Group 10	vs.	Group 12	7	22	144	38	77.0	19.6	-1.988	95.0%
Group 11	vs.	Group 12	7	9	66	25	31.5	9.4	-0.688	50.0%
Group 17	vs.	Group 18	29	30	804	501	435.0	66.0	1.001	60.0%

Mann–Whitney U Test for Calculations of Difference in Sales to Net Worth

Comparison			m	n	T	W	$E(W)$	$SD(W)$	Random Variable	Significance
Group 1	vs.	Group 2	16	27	399	169	216.0	39.8	-1.181	70.0%
Group 1	vs.	Group 3	8	16	98	66	64.0	16.3	0.122	N/S
Group 2	vs.	Group 4	8	27	152	100	108.0	25.5	-0.314	N/S
Group 3	vs.	Group 4	8	8	75	25	32.0	9.5	-0.735	50.0%
Group 13	vs.	Group 14	24	35	783	357	420.0	64.8	-0.972	60.0%
Group 5	vs.	Group 6	14	29	322	189	203.0	38.6	-0.363	N/S
Group 5	vs.	Group 7	9	14	106	65	63.0	15.9	0.126	N/S
Group 6	vs.	Group 8	7	29	140	91	101.5	25.0	-0.420	N/S
Group 7	vs.	Group 8	7	9	53	38	31.5	9.4	0.688	50.0%
Group 15	vs.	Group 16	23	36	709	395	414.0	64.3	-0.295	N/S
Group 9	vs.	Group 10	21	22	524	169	231.0	41.2	-1.506	80.0%
Group 9	vs.	Group 11	9	21	133	101	94.5	22.1	0.294	N/S
Group 10	vs.	Group 12	7	22	117	65	77.0	19.6	-0.612	N/S
Group 11	vs.	Group 12	7	9	53	38	31.5	9.4	0.688	50.0%
Group 17	vs.	Group 18	29	30	797	508	435.0	66.0	1.107	70.0%

BIBLIOGRAPHY

Andrews, K. P. *The Concept of Corporate Strategy*. Homewood, Ill.: Dow Jones-Irwin, Inc., 1971.

Ansoff, H. I. *Corporate Strategy*. New York: McGraw Hill, 1965.

Ansoff, H. I. "Corporate Capability for Managing Change," *SRI Business Intelligence Program, Research Report*, No. 40, Dec. 1978.

Ansoff, H. I. *Strategic Management*. London: MacMillan Press Ltd., 1979.

Ansoff, H. I. *Implanting Strategic Management*. Englewood Cliffs, New Jersey: Prentice-Hall Inc., 1990, 1984.

Ansoff, H. I. "The Emerging Paradigm of Strategic Behavior," *Strategic Management Journal*, 8, No. 6 (1987), pp. 501-515.

Argyris, C. *Integrating the Individual and the Organization*. New York: John Wiley, 1964.

Baughman, J. P. et al. *Environmental Analysis for Management*. Homewood, Ill.: R.D. Irwin, 1974.

Blake, R. R. and J. S. Mouton. *The Managerial Grid*. Houston, Texas: Gulf Publishing Company, 1964.

Bourgois, L. J. "Strategy and Environment: A Conceptual Integration," *Academy of Management Review*, Vol. 5 (1980), pp. 25-39.

Brulton, W. *Business Policy*. New York: MacMillan Publications, Inc., 1984.

Burns, T. and G. M. Stalker. *The Management of Innovation*. London: Tavistock Publications, 1961.

Camillus, J. C. "Reconciling Logical Incrementalism and Synoptic Formalism. An Integrational Approach to Designing Strategic Planning Process," *Strategic Management Journal*, Vol. 3 (1982) pp. 277-283.

Chabane, H. *Restructuring and Performance in Algerian State-Owned Enterprises: A Strategic Management Study*. D.B.A. Dissertation, U.S. International Univerity, San Diego, Cal., 1987.

Chandler, A. D. *Strategy and Structure: Chapters in the History of the American Industrial Enterprise*. Cambridge, Mass.: MIT Press, 1962.

Channon, D. *The Strategy and Structure of British Enterprise*. Boston: Harvard University, 1973.

Child. J. "Organizational Structure, Environment and Performance: The Role of Strategic Choice," *Sociology*, (January 1972), pp. 1-22.

Christensen, R. *Business Policy: Text and Cases*. Homewood, Ill.: R. D. Irwin, 1982.

Cohen, K. and R. Cyert. "Strategy Formulation, Implementation and Monitoring," *The Journal of Business,* Vol. 46 (July 1973), p. 352.

Cosier, R. A. "Dialectical Inquiry in Strategic Planning: A Case of Premature Acceptance," *Academy of Management Review*, (October 1981), pp. 643-648.

Cyert, R. M. and J. G. March. *A Behavioral Theory of the Firm*. Englewood Cliffs, New Jersey: Prentice Hall, Inc., 1963.

Deal, T. E. and A. A. Kennedy. *Corporate Cultures*. Reading, Mass.: Addison-Wesley Publishing Co. Inc., 1982.

Djohar, Setiadi. *The Relationships Between Strategic Effectiveness, Competitive Efficiency, and Performance in Indonesian Firms*. D.B.A. Dissertation, U.S. International University, San Diego, Cal., 1991.

Drucker, P. F. *The Age of Discontinuity*. New York: Harper and Row, 1969.

Drucker, P. F. *Management: Tasks, Responsibilities, Practices*. New York: Harper and Row, 1974.

Drucker, P. F. *Managing in Turbulent Times*. New York: Harper and Row, 1979.

Duncan, R. B. "Characteristics of Organizational Environments and Perceived Environmental Uncertainty," *Administrative Science Quarterly*, Vol. 17 (1972), pp. 313-328.

Emery, F. E. and E. L. Trist. "The Causal Texture of Organizational Environments," *Human Relations*, Vol. 18 (1965), pp. 21-32.

Etzioni, A. *Modern Organizations*. Englewood Cliffs, New Jersey: Prentice Hall, Inc., 1964.

Fombrun, C. J. "Corporate Culture, Environment and Strategy," *Human Resource Management*, Vol. 22 (1983), pp. 139-52.

Galbraith, J. R. *Designing Complex Organizations*. Reading, Mass.: Addison-Wesley, 1973.

Glueck, W. F. *Business Policy*. New York: McGraw-Hill, Inc., 1976.

Glueck, W. F. *Business Policy and Strategic Management*. New York: McGraw Hill, 1984.

Grant, J. H. and W. R. King. *The Logic of Strategic Planning*. Boston: Little Brown and Company, 1982.

Harris P. R. and R. T. Moran. *Managing Cultural Differences*. Houston, Texas: Gulf Publishing Co., 1979.

Hersberg, F. *Work and the Nature of Man*. London: Staples Press, 1968.

Higgins, R. B. "Long Range Planning in the Mature Organization," *Strategic Management Journal*, (July-September 1981), pp. 235-250.

Hodgetts, R. M. *Administrative Policy: Text and Cases in Strategic Management*. New York: John Wiley.

Hofer, C. W., E. A. Murray, Jr., P. Charan and R. Pitts. *Strategic Management. A Casebook in Policy and Planning*. Santa Clara, Cal.: West Publishing Co., 1984.

Jaja, R.M. *Technology and Banking: The Implication of Technological Change on the Financial Performance of Commercial Banks*. D.B.A. Dissertation, U.S. International University, San Diego, Cal., 1990.

Jurkovitch, R. "A Core Typology of Organization Environments," *Administrative Science Quarterly*, Vol. 19 (1974), pp. 380-394.

Key Business Ratios. New York: Dun and Bradstreet, Inc., 1969-1985.

King, W. R. and D. I. Cleland. "Environmental Information Systems for Strategic Marketing Planning," *Journal of Marketing*, (October 1974), pp. 35-40.

King, W. R., B. K. Dutta and J. T. Rodriquez. "Strategic Competitive Information Systems," *OMEGA*, (April 1978), pp. 123-132.

King, W. R. and J. T. Rodriquez. "Participative Design of Strategic Design Support Systems: An Empirical Assessment," *Management Science*, (June 1981), p. 717-726.

Leavitt, H. *Managerial Psychology*. Chicago: The University of Chicago Press, Ltd., 1964.

Leontiades, J. *Strategies for Diversification and Change*. Boston: Little Brown, 1980.

Lewis, A.O. *Strategic Posture and Financial Performance of the Banking Industry in California: A Strategic Management Study*. D.B.A. Dissertation, U.S. International University, San Diego, Cal., 1989.

Likert, R. *The Human Organization: Its Management and Value*. New York: McGraw-Hill, 1967.

Linsay, W. M. and L. W. Rue. "Impact of the Business Environment On Long Range Planning Process: A Contingency View." *Academy of Management Proceedings*, (1978), pp. 116-120.

McNichols, T. J. *Executive Policy and Strategic Planning*. New York: McGraw-Hill, 1977.

McNichols, T. J. *Policy Making and Executive Action*. New York: McGraw-Hill, 1963.

March, J. G. and H. A. Simon. *Organizations*. New York: Wiley, 1958.

Miles, R. E., C. C. Snow and J. Pfeffer. "Organization Environment: Concepts and Issues," *Industrial Relations*, (October 1974), pp. 244-266.

Mintzberg, H. *The Nature of Managerial Work*. New York: Harper and Row, 1973.

Mintzberg, H. *The Structuring of Organizations*. Englewood Cliffs, New Jersey: Prentice-Hall, Inc., 1979.

Mitroff, I. I. and J. R. Emshoff. "On Strategic Assumption-Making: A Dialectical Approach to Policy and Planning," *Academy of Management Review*, (October 1979), pp. 1-12.

Mitiku, A. *The Relationship of General Management Capability with Performance in State-Owned Industrial Enterprises in Ethiopia: A Strategic Approach*. D.B.A. Dissertation, U.S. International University, San Diego, Cal., 1991.

Moody's Industrial Manual. New York: Moody's Investor's Service Inc., 1971-1981.

Naumes, W. and F. T. Paine. *Cases for Organizational Strategy and Policy*. Philadelphia: W. B. Saunders Company, 1978.

Peters, T. J. "The Rational Model Has Led Us Astray," *Planning Review*, (March 1982), pp. 16-23.

Peters, T. F. and R. J. Waterman, Jr. *In Search of Excellence*. New York: Harper and Row, 1982.

Peters, T. F. *Thriving on Chaos*, New York: Alfred A. Knopf, Inc., 1987.

Pettigrew, A. M. "On Studying Organizational Cultures," *Administrative Science Quarterly*, Vol. 24, (1979), pp. 570-581.

Quinn, J. B. "Managing Strategic Change," *Sloan Management Review*, (Summer 1980), pp. 3-20.

Quinn, J. B. *Strategies for Change: Logical Incrementalism*. Homewood, Ill.: Irwin, Inc., 1980.

Radford, J.K. *Strategic Planning: An Analytical Approach*. Englewood Cliffs, New Jersey: Prentice Hall, 1980.

Rhyne, L. C. "The Relationship of Information Usage Characteristics to Planning Systems Sophistication: An Empirical Examination," *Strategic Management Journal*, Vol. 6, (1985), pp. 319-337.

Rummelt, R. P. *Strategy, Structure and Economic Performance*. Boston Graduate School: Harvard University, 1974.

Salameh, T. T. *Strategic Posture Analysis and Financial Performance of the Banking Industry in U.A.E.: A Strategic Management Study*. D.B.A. Dissertation, U.S. International Univerisity, San Diego, Cal., 1987.

Schein, E. H. *Organizational Psychology*. Englewood Cliffs, NJ: Prentice-Hall, Inc., 1970.

Schein, E. H. "The Role of the Founder in Creating Organizational Culture," *Organizational Dynamics*, (Summer 1983), pp. 13-28.

Siehl, C. and J. Martin. "Learning Organizational Culture," *Working Paper*, Graduate School of Business, Stanford University, (1981).

Silverman, D. *A Theory of Organizations*. London: Heineman Educational Books, 1970.

Sloan, A. P., Jr. *My Years With General Motors*. Garden City, New York: Doubleday and Company, Inc., 1972.

Spradley, J. P. and D. W. McCurdy. *Anthropology: The Cultural Perspective*. New York: John Wiley, 1975.

Steers, R. M. *Organizational Effectiveness: A Behavioral View*. Santa Monica, Cal.: Goodyear Publishing Co., 1977.

Steiner, G. A. *Top Management Planning*. New York: MacMillan, 1969.

Steiner, G. A. *Management Policy and Strategy*. New York: MacMillan Publishing Co., Inc., 1977.

Steiner, G. A. *Strategic Planning: What Every Manager Must Know*. New York: MacMillan Publishing Co., Inc., 1979.

Steiner, G. A. "A New Class of C.E.O.," *Long Range Planning*, (August 1981), pp. 10-20.

Steiner, G. A. *Management Policy and Strategy*. New York: MacMillan Publishing Co., Inc., 1982.

Steiner, G. A. "Formal Strategic Planning in the United States Today," *Long Range Planning*, (June 1983), pp. 12-27.

Sullivan, P.A. *The Relationship Between Proportion of Income Derived from Subsidy and Strategic Performance of a Federal Agency Under the Commercial Activities Program*. D.B.A. Dissertation, U.S. International University, San Diego, Cal., 1987.

Summer, C. E. *Strategic Behavior in Business and Government*. Boston: Little Brown and Company, 1980.

Tichy, N. "The Essentials of Strategic Change Management," *The Journal of Business Strategy*, Vol. 3 (1983), pp. 55-67.

Thompson, A. A., Jr. *Strategy and Policy, Concepts and Cases*. Dallas, Texas: Business Publications Inc., 1978.

Thompson, A. A., Jr. and A. J. Strickland, III. *Strategic Management: Concepts and Cases*. Dallas, Texas: Business Publications Inc., 1984.

Thompson, J. *Organizations in Action*. New York: McGraw Hill, 1967.

Thorelli, H. B. *Strategy + Structure = Performance*. Blomington, Indiana: University Press, 1977.

Uyterhoven, H. E. Strategy and Organization. *Text and Cases in General Management*. Homewood, Ill.: R. D. Irwin., 1977.

Wang, Pien. *Determinants of Perception of Environmental Turbulence and Strategic Responses of Savings and Loan Top Managers*. D.B.A. Dissertation, U.S. International University, San Diego, Cal., 1991.

Werner, O., M. Topper and Associates. *Handbook of Ethnoscience: Ethnographies and Encyclopedia*. Evanston, Ill.: Department of Anthropology, Northwest University, 1979.

Wheelen, T. L. and J. D. Hunger. *Strategic Management and Business Policy*. Reading, Penn.: Addison-Wesley Publishing Co., Inc., 1983.

Wrapp, H. E. "Good Managers Don't Make Policy Decisions," *Harvard Business Review*, (September 1967), pp. 91-99.

INDEX

 The Planning Forum

The Planning Forum is the world's leading international business organization focused on advancing the understanding and practice of strategic management as the integrating force for improving organizational performance and achieving global competitiveness. Our publications, programs and member network of over 6,000 business executives worldwide provide access to the top thought-leaders in the field and enhance strategic thinking, learning and networking.

Services include the annual International Strategic Management Conference; regional educational conferences; monthly meetings at 44 chapters across North America; Research and Education Foundation; *Planning Review* magazine, the top-rated business-oriented publication in the strategic management and planning field; a 2,000-plus volume members-only research library; and *Network,* an award-winning monthly executive briefing.

For membership information, contact The Planning Forum at:

5500 College Corner Pike
P.O. Box 70
Oxford, OH 45056
Phone: (513) 523-4185
Fax: (513) 523-7539